Glendale College
Library

THE FUTURE
OF IMPRISONMENT

STUDIES IN CRIME AND JUSTICE

THE FUTURE OF IMPRISONMENT

Norval Morris

THE UNIVERSITY OF CHICAGO PRESS
Chicago and London

365
Mor

The University of Chicago Press, Chicago 60637
The University of Chicago Press, Ltd., London

© 1974 by The University of Chicago
All rights reserved. Published 1974
Printed in the United States of America

Library of Congress Cataloging in Publication Data

Morris, Norval.
    The future of imprisonment.

    (Studies in crime and justice)
    "Revised and expanded version of the Thomas M. Cooley
lectures offered at the University of Michigan Law
School in March 1974."
    Bibliography: p.
    1. Imprisonment. 2. Prisons. I. Title.
II. Series. III. Series: Michigan. University.
Law School. The Thomas M. Cooley lectures.
HV8705.M67   365   74–13920
ISBN 0–226–53905–9 [clothbound]

Per stirpes et per connubia felicia
To Christopher, Deborah, Gareth, Malcolm,
and Susan

Contents

Preface

Prisons have few friends; dissatisfaction with them is widespread. They are too frequently the scene of brutality, violence, and racial conflict. And insofar as prisons purport to cure criminals of crime, their record has not been encouraging. Nevertheless, prisons have other purposes—to punish, to deter, to banish—which assure their continued survival.

This likely continuance of imprisonment does not preclude a profound evolutionary change in what is a "prison." The size and situation of the typical American prison certainly should change, its population should be selected by less discriminatory means, and its social processes require massive reordering. But the paths to these and other prison reforms are neither clear nor agreed upon.

Prison is, in practice, the ultimate power the democratic state exercises over a citizen, yet we lack a jurisprudence of imprisonment. This book is an attempt to define the proper role of the prison in a democratic society. Principles are proposed by which what is of value in the "rehabilitative ideal" within prisons may be retained, while the present corruptive effects of compulsory rehabilitative programs may be eliminated. Principles are also offered to decide who should be in prison and for what purposes.

The search is for a new model of imprisonment that provides for the legitimate exercise of society's power over the convicted criminal and protects fundamental principles of justice. It is a jurisprudential model rather than an operational model; the discussion is more of the forces that shape the prison than of the operation of the prison community, though the two are, of course, intertwined.

In the fourth chapter, the principles enunciated in the first three are applied to the design of a prison for repetitively violent criminals and an evaluative scheme is suggested by which those principles might be critically tested.

A survey of the major features of the terrain to be traversed may assist the reader either to avoid the journey or to follow the paths later delineated.

The propositions are unargued; qualifications are left to the text.

—Prison as a punishment for serious crime was invented in America in the last quarter of the eighteenth century. Its inventors intended one of its purposes to be to cure criminals of crime.

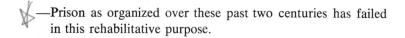

—Prison as organized over these past two centuries has failed in this rehabilitative purpose.

—There is widespread criticism of the prison, yet its population remains stable and substantial in this and other countries.

—Frequently suggested means of reducing imprisonment, by diversions to community-based treatments, are unlikely to be successful until principles are defined and broadly agreed on for the imposition of imprisonment. We must be clear who should go to prison, not merely who should not.

—Rehabilitative programs in prison must be expanded and improved but they must be related neither to the time the prisoner serves nor to the conditions of his incarceration. Prison training and treatment programs must be entirely facilitative, never imposed.

—If a fixed prison sentence has not been imposed, the prisoner must be advised, within a few weeks of sentencing, of the date of his parole.

—Graduated testing of increased increments of freedom must be substituted for parole predictions of suitability for release.

—Present sentencing practices are so arbitrary, discriminatory, and unprincipled that it is impossible to build a rational and humane prison system on them.

—"Plea bargaining" is at present an unavoidable expedient; but it can be made into a principled and just system of sentencing if the proper interests, including those of the victim, are represented at pretrial dispositional hearings.

—Principles guiding the decision to imprison should be these:
1. *Parsimony:* the least restrictive (punitive) sanction necessary to achieve defined social purposes should be imposed.
2. *Dangerousness:* prediction of future criminality should be rejected as a base for determining that the convicted criminal should be imprisoned.
3. *Desert:* no sanction should be imposed greater than that which is "deserved" by the last crime, or series of crimes, for which the offender is being sentenced.

—Preconditions to imprisonment are these (they are conjunctive):

> A. Conviction by jury or bench trial or an acceptable plea of guilty to an offense for which imprisonment is legislatively prescribed.
>
> *and*
>
> B. Imprisonment is the least restrictive (punitive) sanction appropriate in this case because:
>
> > *either*   i) any lesser punishment would depreciate the seriousness of the crime(s) committed,
> >
> > *or*   ii) imprisonment of some who have done what this criminal did is necessary to achieve socially justified deterrent purposes, and the punishment of this offender is an appropriate vehicle to that end,
> >
> > *or*   iii) other less restrictive sanctions have been applied to this offender frequently or recently.
>
> *and*
>
> C. Imprisonment is not a punishment which would be seen by current mores as undeserved (excessive) in relation to the last crime or series of crimes.

—Finally, an operational design of an institution for two hundred repetitively violent criminals is offered in which some of the principles recommended in this book could be critically tested in practice.

Acknowledgments

This book is a revised and expanded version of the Thomas M. Cooley Lectures offered at the University of Michigan Law School in March 1974. I am grateful to the University of Michigan Law School for this stimulus and to my own Law School at the University of Chicago for lightening my teaching load so that I might better respond to Michigan's helpful prodding.

Some of the ideas in the first two chapters were tested in the Sir John Barry Memorial Lecture offered in Melbourne, Australia, in July 1973. It was a privilege to speak in memory of a great Australian judge, also an eminent historian of the criminal law, who uniquely combined high scholarly values with an earthy judicial realism.

Scholarship is dependent. I have been most fortunate in my colleagues in the universities that have employed me. They were my daily teachers. There are many to whom I owe gratitude, but, if a short list has to be made, there are unrepayable debts to Francis Allen, the late Sir John Barry, Gordon Hawkins, Colin Howard, the late Hermann Mannheim, Hans W. Mattick, Sir George Paton, Georg Stürup, and Franklin Zimring.

I am deeply indebted to Gordon Hawkins and Franklin Zimring for their generous and perceptive work on successive drafts of this book. I am also very grateful to Marian Badger, Jim Jacobs, Ben Meeker, Bernard Rubin, and Eric Steele, who were a year-long source of creative ideas on the proposed prison for repetitively violent criminals and who played a major role in shaping the fourth chapter.

The Department of Corrections of Illinois collaborated in the planning for the institution for repetitively violent criminals. We were funded by a federal Law Enforcement Assistance Administration discretionary grant channeled through the Illinois Law Enforcement Commission, with William Craine and Arthur Huffman at different stages collaborating with me in directing this project. I am appreciative of their assistance. The administrative complexities of such arrangements, involving several state and federal bureaucracies, are far from inconsequential: they were handled with quiet efficiency by Leonard Lieberman, who also contributed many substantive ideas to the project.

Lloyd Ohlin, Milton Rector, and Georg Stürup served as the Dean's "hired guns" at Ann Arbor, enlivening the Cooley Lectures and helping me in this revision by forceful criticism of my model of imprisonment.

To have a volume of my own in the Studies in Crime and Justice series, when I serve on its editorial board, is a particular pleasure. It allows me the opportunity to express my appreciation to the B. E. Bensinger family for their generous financial support of this series, and to my friend Peter Bensinger for his energetic dedication to the considerable tasks of bringing decency and efficiency to the prisons of Illinois and the criminal justice systems of Cook County.

The University of Chicago Press provided its usual blend of insightful encouragement and brutal criticism in which any author of not too sensitive hide will rejoice.

The Regenstein Library provided a sparsely furnished, well-lit, isolated, and silent, 9′ x 6′ cell, proximate to the literature and ideal for reflection and writing on imprisonment.

1   Prison as Coerced Cure

The present intellectual climate is uncongenial to rational speculation directed to social change. There is a pervading sense of rudderlessness, of being the captives of social forces beyond our control. We have seen so many apparently sound reforms drowned in the complex crosscurrents of sectional interest and political myopia. Daniel Boorstin put it precisely in his *The Americans: The Democratic Experience:* "Now the American assignment seemed to come no longer from the conscious choices of individual citizens, but from the scale and velocity of the national projects themselves. . . . Man's problem of self-determination was more baffling than ever. For the very power of the most democratized nation on earth had led its citizens to feel inconsequential before the forces they had unleashed" (p. 558).

Hence, I approach with hesitance the task of rational planning for the future of imprisonment. The momentum of futility and brutality in imprisonment is great; the political forces obstructing change are deeply entrenched; and the reformers have no agreed-upon program. They may sometimes concur on what is wrong but they lack the inner compass of shared principles to chart a path to other than ameliorative change. There is a

1

fervor and factionalism, a modishness, in their recommendations that seriously impede correctional reform.

Further, I recognize that my effort to offer and to analyze general principles under which imprisonment may be part of a rational criminal justice system will be attacked from the right as too permissive and idealistic and from the left as too punitive and opportunistic. Nevertheless, reform requires more than agreement on the immediate and pragmatic if prison is to be used in the future—and it seems to me highly likely that prison will be used in the future.

Until quite recently I had seen the subject of this book as epiphenomenal, even to the criminal law, and certainly as lying outside the central problems of society. But I have come to wonder about that; perhaps it is a fundamental issue. Solzhenitsyn's work *The Gulag Archipelago* is obviously seen by the Russian authorities as no trivial challenge to the political order. Similarly, the proper role of imprisonment as a sanction for criminal behavior reaches to the top—at any rate, warmly close to the top—of political organization in this country. Prison is, after all, the largest power that the state exercises in practice, on a regular basis, over its citizens—though the anachronism of capital punishment persists in some places as a rarely invoked return to barbarism. Perhaps if we can bring principle and justice to the exercise of the power of imprisonment, much else will improve in the uneasy tension between freedom and authority in post-industrial society. With the increasing tenuousness and vulnerability of our social organization and the growing complexity and interdependence of governmental structures, a reassessment of the proper limits to the power that society should exercise over its members becomes a fundamental concern. That question is beyond my purpose, but to address it in one context—the proper use of imprisonment as a criminal sanction—may contribute to the larger analysis.

Prisons provide widely diverse conditions, from comfortable, relaxed environments to stews of suffering. In common is the sense of banishment, but little else. Let me sketch polarities I have observed. At one end is a Fiji prison, with the prisoners working relatively unsupervised on the docks. At five o'clock the prison bell rings. A wild scurrying, pell-mell toward the iron gates of the prison, which clang shut five minutes after the bell, it being well understood that any prisoner locked out will get no dinner that night and will on no account be allowed in until the next morning! By contrast, the prison's prison in an American mega-prison: the punishment cell, isolation, the hole, is the prison's prison. And sometimes there is even the prison's prison's prison—the strip cell, dark, silent, steel-plated, quite unfurnished for the triply punished.

To offer general principles for the reform of such diverse institutions, to predict their future, is no small task; but prediction does not necessarily involve self-deception. At all events, it may help to carry discussion beyond the present polar dogmatisms of the punishers of crime, with their mindless reliance on the prison, and the curers of criminals, with their boundless confidence in the enforceability of the Sermon on the Mount.

Observation of many prisons in many countries informs this book; but travel may broaden the posterior more than the mind, and I make no claim that restless wandering can substitute for thought. Still, occasionally it produces a flash of insight. One such came when visiting Dachau. I was advised that that memorial to man's frenzied cruelty to man started as a model prison—a small institution of modest security, close to a charming town, where small groups of malleable prisoners were to be held in clean and attractive surroundings. And it was to be a model institution in another sense—it was to be used also for the training of correctional officers. Not a whip in mind; not an oven in sight. But the decline to nightmare, the plunge through the circles of hell, was precipitate.

It is not, I think, menopausal depression that leads me to believe that the proper use of imprisonment as a penal sanction is of central practical and theoretical importance to the future of social organization generally. From such large pretensions, let me turn to the subject of this book—the future of imprisonment.

The Historical Base

If past is prologue, prediction requires a historical base. The history of imprisonment has often been told and will not here be fully rehearsed; a brief sketch should suffice. Punitive imprisonment as a part of slave labor was used extensively in ancient Rome, Egypt, China, India, Assyria, and Babylon, and was firmly established in Europe by the Renaissance. As a penal sanction—as distinct from its age-old and worldwide use to detain the accused until trial or the convicted criminal until punishment—imprisonment has also been widely applied to the mass of petty offenders, vagrants, alcoholics, mentally ill, inadequate nuisances, and sturdy beggars in most societies. Nevertheless, until quite recently the serious offender, other than the political criminal, was not imprisoned as a penal sanction. He may have been penned for other purposes but not imprisoned as a punishment. Felons were dealt with by exile, banishment, transportation, and a diversity of demeaning and painful corporal punishments—the "cat," the ear and nose cropper, the branding iron, and that reliable standby, capital punishment. Prisons for felons arose as a reaction to the excesses and barbarisms of earlier punishments; imprisonment was one of the early "diversions" from traditional criminal sanctions.

The jail, the workhouse, the almshouse, the reformatory, and the convict ship all antedate the prison. The castle keep for the political personage out of favor or office and the church's cell for retreat and penance were part of the genesis of the prison, but they were established for different social classes and different political purposes. What is sometimes forgotten, although unkindly reminders have lately become fashionable, is that the prison is an American invention, an invention of the Pennsylvania Quakers of the last decade of the eighteenth century, though one might also note the confining "People Pen" put up by the Massachusetts Pilgrims nearly two centuries earlier (Jordan, 1970, pp. 140–54). In their "penitentiary" the Quakers planned to substitute the correctional specifics of isolation, repentance, and the uplifting effects of scriptural injunctions and solitary Bible reading for the brutality and inutility of capital and corporal punishments. These three treatments—removal from corrupting peers, time for reflection and self-examination, the guidance of biblical precepts—would no doubt have been helpful to the reflective Quakers who devised the prison, but relatively few of them ever became prisoners. The suitability of these remedies for the great mass of those who subsequently found their way to the penitentiary is more questionable.

The Pennsylvania Quakers found theoretical direction for the penitentiary not only in their own theological and moral beliefs but also in Beccaria's monograph *On Crimes and Punishments*, published in 1764. The thrust of his argument for prisons has a modern counterpart: To Beccaria the prison was the necessary alternative to capital punishment; it was, in modern terminology, a diversion from the established criminal justice system. He rarely mentions imprisonment except as a substitute for execution.

At all events, in 1790 a cell block was opened in the Walnut Street Jail of Philadelphia as the "penitentiary" for the Commonwealth of Pennsylvania. In 1796, Newgate began service as the penitentiary for the State of New York, modeled on the Walnut Street Jail but taking its name from an earlier English institution serving a different clientele (civil and criminal debtors and those awaiting trial or punishment).

Prisons grew and flourished throughout America and later throughout the world; they are a pervasive American export, like tobacco in their international acceptance and perhaps also in their adverse consequences. The Pennsylvania Quakers must be praised or blamed for the invention or reinvention of the prison. Their vision and initiative gave us our hulking penal institutions, our "edifice complex." It was a gift born of benevolence not malevolence, of philanthrophy not punitiveness, so that the most important contemporary lesson of this historical sketch may well be a deeper appreciation of the truth that benevolent intentions do not necessarily produce beneficent results.

Abolition or Abatement of Imprisonment

Contemporary Quakers in the American Friends Service Committee's book, *Struggle for Justice*, recognize that "the horror that is the American prison system grew out of an 18th Century reform" proposed by their ideological forebears. Their criticism is of a cruelty characteristic of intrafamilial disputes, but they are by no means alone in their castigation of imprisonment. From John Bartlow Martin to Jessica Mitford a popular prison abolitionist literature has grown, and scholars have been hardly less critical. Both national crime commissions of the past decade recommended the swift abatement of imprisonment, and the 1973 commission urged a moratorium on the construction of all new institutions for adult or juvenile offenders, a position also adopted by the National Council on Crime and Delinquency. Judge James E. Doyle, a federal district court judge of the Western District of Wisconsin, was formidably direct in the matter. In *Morales v. Schmidt*, a prison mail censorship case, he said: "I am persuaded that the institution of prison probably must end. In many respects it is as intolerable within the United States as was the institution of slavery, equally brutalizing to all involved, equally toxic to the social system, equally subversive of the brotherhood of man, even more costly by some standard, and probably less rational" (340 F. Supp. 544, 548–49 [W. D. Wis. 1972], rev'd. [7th Cir. 1973]).

The 1973 national commission, the National Advisory Commission on Criminal Justice Standards and Goals, recommended that "the institution should be the last resort for correctional problems" (Corrections Task Force, p. 2), gave their reasons—failure to reduce crime, success in punishing but not in deterring, providing only a temporary protection to the community, changing the offender but mostly for the worse—and concluded that "the prison . . . has persisted, partly because a civilized nation could neither turn back to the barbarism of an earlier time nor find a satisfactory alternative" (ibid., p. 343).

There would seem to be agreement among scholars, commentators, and certainly vocal prisoners that radical change leading to a new model of imprisonment is urgently needed. Imprisonment has been too much used, it has discriminated against races and classes, sentences imposed have been too long, and too many of them have been served in degrading and brutalizing circumstances. There is widespread advocacy of a swift abatement if not an abolition of imprisonment. How is this to be achieved?

The Paths to Abatement of Imprisonment

Three paths are believed to lead to the abatement of imprisonment. First, the "overreach" of the criminal law is to be reduced. Second, those who would otherwise be sent to prison are to be "diverted" to other mechanisms of social control. And third, greater reliance is to be placed on "community-based corrections." These three amount to defining less behavior as criminal, keeping an increasing proportion of offenders out of prison, and getting an increasing proportion out of prison earlier than at present; all groups so liberated to be controlled and supported in a variety of treatment programs in the community. There is a widespread realization that both the criminal prohibition and the penal institution have been used indiscriminately and excessively.

The criminal law's reach has been extended in this country far beyond its competence, invading the spheres of private morality and social welfare, proving ineffective, corruptive, and criminogenic. This overreach of the criminal law has made hypocrites of us all and has cluttered the courts and filled the jails and prisons, the detention centers and reformatories, with people who should not be there. Regulatory systems, backed by the criminal sanction if regulations are flouted, should be substituted for the mass of prohibitory propositions at present brought to bear on a wide swath of behavior. Though much of what now busies the criminal justice system may be immoral or troublesome or distasteful or unseemly or injurious to the actor and to those who love him or depend on him, it does not represent a serious threat to the physical safety of others nor a major depredation to property nor a serious challenge to governmental authority. The criminal law of the future will work more as an administrative law of crime, backing up licensing and regulatory systems, than as a clumsy scheme of direct prohibitions.

We gradually learn to be more discriminating and selective in using penal sanctions in that wide area of human behavior where no citizen identifies himself as a victim, where no complainant seeks to invoke criminal law processes. For example, there is a strong legislative and judicial trend toward the decriminalization of drug addiction itself and what is supposed to be the nonpunitive treatment of the addict, balanced by more forceful crime control efforts directed against the professional vendor of drugs. Similar legislative and judicial tendencies are to be seen in relation to gambling, public drunkenness, and a variety of sexual gaieties and exuberances.

Just as there has been an overemphasis on the use of the prohibitory sanctions of the criminal law, so there has been an overemphasis on custody. It is widely recognized that we have locked up too many social nuisances who are not social threats, too many petty offenders and minor thieves, severing such few social ties as they have and pushing them further toward more serious criminal behavior. This excessive use of incarceration, the prison and the jail, the reformatory and the detention center, has been expensive, criminogenic, and unkind. Hence, increasingly we try to "divert" different categories of offenders from the criminal justice system and from penal institutions.

Diversions from the criminal justice system and from prisons grow apace at the police, prosecutorial, and judicial levels. Police diversions to mental health, social welfare, and addiction treatment units reduce the flow to prison as do judicial and prosecutorial diversions to probationary and similar supervisory and supportive services.

There is also support for increased reliance on the fine and on restitution and compensation payments to the victims of crime as an alternative to imprisonment. This is a wholly sound development which should be extended by the adoption of systems like the Swedish "day fine" and time payment arrangements adjusted to the economic realities of the lives of convicted persons.

Despite these movements, the prison population remains stable at about the 200,000 mark (I do not count the jails), though an increased proportion of convicted offenders are on probation, in "halfway" houses and probation hostels, and in other community based treatments.

There are further trends toward the abatement of imprisonment. Recent criminal codes, federal and state, try both to bring order and equity to the lottery of sentencing and to reduce the duration of prison terms. There are exceptions, such as New York's legislation concerning the sale of hard drugs and the similar federal proposal for life terms for pushers, but the general legislative and judicial tendency is toward shorter prison terms.

Within the terms of imprisonment imposed, there is a growing and determined effort to break down the prison walls in the sense that the walls keep community influences out. It is recognized that every effort must be made to preserve any social ties the prisoner may have. Hence, restrictions are fewer on regular visiting, censorship of prisoner's mail is ending (though selective inspection of incoming mail for drugs and contraband remains necessary), facilities for telephone calls by prisoners are being installed, regular furlough programs are beginning, and use of work release, halfway houses, pre-release hostel placements, and other graduated release facilities is increasing. There emerges a serious commitment, particularly for the bulk of less threatening prisoners, to the reduction of their social isolation. Finally, few voices are raised in favor of retaining the megaprisons that still typify American corrections. There is agreement, qualified only by some irresponsible cries for the establishment of "maxi-maxi security" institutions, about substituting for them, for that proportion of the criminal population that will require incarceration, small multi-purpose institutions close to the cities and towns where most of the inmates will live after their release.

The Dangers of Diversion

There is a persistent human tendency to believe that all social problems are soluble and that one way or another the undesirable behavior of others can be coercively changed; indeed, in this country to define a problem is seen as the mere preamble to its solution. Regretfully, but with determination, I must express a qualification to too ready an acceptance of the beneficence of these movements toward reducing the reach of the criminal law and abating imprisonment by the means of diversion from the criminal justice system. It seems to me that these processes will be accompanied by an increase in the number of citizens who are brought under social control.

A threshold definitional problem may be resolved by fiat. As used in this analysis, "diversion" from the criminal justice system is always conditional. If a policeman or prosecutor or judge or parole officer decides to take no further action at all in relation to the suspect or to the convicted criminal, it is to be regarded as an "exclusion" from the criminal justice system even if a record of the encounter is kept. This distinction is essential to the argument.

It will be recalled that in Orwell's dark disutopia, *1984*, the criminal law, quite unlike the state, had indeed withered away. The Ministry of Love—Miniluv—was in charge of discordant,

aberrant, and socially injurious behavior. A wide variety of
social controls, techniques of observation and overhearing,
subtle methods of encouraging and influencing behavior, were
substituted for the clumsy prohibitions and punishments of the
criminal law. Few escaped their influence. The present danger
is that the regulatory and licensing techniques that will sup-
plant the overreaching criminal law in the areas of complaint-
less crimes, and the diversionary techniques that will protect
offenders from the greater rigors of imprisonment, may lead to
a substantial extension of social control by official state processes rather than to a reduction. We face a difficult trade-off.
We risk substituting more pervasive but less punitive control
mechanisms over a vastly larger number of citizens for our
present discriminatory and irrational selection of fewer citizens
for more punitive and draconian punishments.

The consequential increase in the numbers under control can
be easily demonstrated. If for a given suspected crime the police
have a choice of arresting or not and are given, by legislation
or administrative authority, a further discretion to issue a summons or notice to appear, then fewer suspected criminals will
be arrested but more will reach the courts. The group given
summons or notices to appear will reduce both the number
arrested and the number whose behavior for a variety of reasons
does not lead to their arrest; the proportion that confront the
court will increase. Or to take another more typical diversionary program, consider the Manhattan Court Employment Project by which selected persons accused within defined categories
of misdemeanor and felony are offered postponement of court
action if they enter the project, and dismissal of charges if they
succeed in a treatment program of group therapy and employment counseling. Not unexpectedly, those presenting the least
threat to the community among the arraigned defendants are so
"diverted." In the result, "the degree of supervision and treatment is greater in the project than it would have been if they
had stayed in the criminal justice system" (Zimring, 1973, p.
24; "Measuring the Impact of Pretrial Diversion . . . ," 1974).

The point is of general significance and fundamental. A stu-
dent with prosecutorial experience put it aphoristically, if ex-
aggeratedly, to me: "The guilty we convict; the innocent we
divert and supervise." Such is the coercive threat of trial, the

pain of detention, the delays, the fears and uncertainties of punishment, that diversionary processes prove compelling for all but the most determinedly innocent or the most experienced in crime. The juvenile court itself was a diversionary program, aiming to reduce the impact of the criminal law on the young offender and to divert him to less punitive, rehabilitative controls. It has swept more children within the ambit of the criminal law than if the state had not gone coercively into the business of child saving by means of statutes ill defining delinquency. Likewise, probation reduces the proportion of convicted offenders in prison but increases the total number under the control of the criminal justice system. The same tendency is apparent in our coercive diversions of addicts and public drunks to narcotic treatment centers and detoxification facilities. The same principle is exemplified in the use of parole as another type of conditional diversion from prison; it may be, though this is in doubt, that parole has tended overall to reduce the actual time served in prison, but it has certainly, at any one time, increased the number of convicted offenders under control.

This trade-off of diversion, reducing the intensity and severity of control but increasing the numbers under control, has a further complexity which cannot be burked, though it is barely noticed in the literature. Conditional diversions always tend to require support for *and* supervision of the offender; and this possibly dysfunctional conjunction of roles is usually given to one supervisor-treater. In the result there is a strong tendency to increase sharply the range and severity of compulsory controls over the criminals diverted from prison. "The desire to help, when coupled with the desire to control, is totalitarian" (Greenberg, "Rehabilitation Is Still Punishment," 1972, p. 28). Consider such wholly well-motivated and closely studied California programs as the Probation Subsidy Program and the Community Treatment Project. These diversions have reduced the proportion of offenders in prisons and reformatories in California and have increased the numbers under control, but there is a further unanticipated development. Increasingly, in both programs, temporary or short-term detention is used as part of the community-based controls. Jails and local detention centers provide, in both programs, periods of temporary or "therapeutic detention" (their phrase). Of a randomly selected group of youths diverted from institutional placement, it was found that the average number of "therapeutic detentions" for each youth in the community treatment project was 2.8 and the average length of stay in custody was 20 days on each such occasion—a total of 56 days of confinement each. The lesser controls of diversionary programs may not be all that mild; intermittent imprisonment may be substituted for a longer single stretch in the slammer.

Finally on the dangers of diversion, it is important that we do not unthinkingly substitute medical models for criminal law models. We must recognize that coercive treatment itself may be quite ineffective. And this may be true both in community-based treatment to which the offender is diverted and in rehabilitative treatment within the prison, to which we shall now return.

Prison as Coerced Cure

Optimism is an unfashionable intellectual posture. Gloomy foreboding, buttressed by analytical demolition of accepted doctrine, is a surer path to academic reputation. Nevertheless, I wish to argue an optimistic view of the future of imprisonment in which the prison retains an important residual role in the criminal justice system. Bravely, I speak up for the accepted. Despite scholarly attacks, despite assaults by national commissions, despite even the powerful criticisms of prisoners, the prison has, in my view, a considerable future which merits rational analysis and careful planning.

I am confirmed in persevering in this foolhardy effort to define both a proper role for the prison and an appropriate function for rehabilitative purposes within the prison by what seem to me two obvious realities. First, the prison shows no sign of disappearing anywhere in the world. True, in Holland, fewer than fifty prisoners per hundred thousand of population are to be found, but Holland has long enjoyed a lesser rate of incarceration than any other country civilized enough to have a prison. And allied to this worldwide application of imprisonment in widely diverse societies is the fact that, somewhat unexpectedly, crime rates and rates of imprisonment move over time independently of one another (Christie, 1968; Blumstein, 1973). The use of the prison, it seems, responds to a variety of pressures in society other than the rate of crime. If these pressures lead, as they do in all countries, to a collection of prisoners who, disproportionately to other social groups, are unemployed, vocationally untrained, undereducated, psychologically disturbed, and socially isolated, it is both humane and in the community's best interests to help them to remedy these deficiencies.

Second, I am encouraged to try to save something of the rehabilitative ideal, despite the activist legions massed behind Francis Allen (1964) in his assault on it, by speculating who would staff prisons that lacked entirely any rehabilitative aspirations. The job of a turnkey, with no possibility of assistance to his charges in refashioning their often shattered lives, would be particularly unattractive; the staff recruited would reflect the dull routine of merely custodial function. It is pointless to deny outlet to the staff's inclination, where it exists or can be mobilized, to help those committed to their care.

Rehabilitative programs in prisons have been characterized more by false rhetoric than by solid achievement (Wootton, 1959; Martinson, 1974). They have been corrupted to punitive purposes. But it does not follow that they should be discarded.

I do not lightly brush aside the argument against the rehabilitative ideal since that "ideal," like the prison, is under massive attack. The concept of individualized treatment as a correctional purpose is rejected by thoughtful and influential students of corrections and my tentative speculation about the needs of prisoners and of the prison staff will not suffice, unsupported, to the contrary. The issue demands a more careful analysis.

Rehabilitation: From Coerced Cure to Facilitated Change

The principal purposes of pre-nineteenth-century punishment were retribution and deterrence, special and general. By intimidation or incapacitation the offender would be persuaded or compelled not to do it again. Compelled?—the handless make poor pickpockets and the executed inept murderers. The example of their suffering would diminish crime by leading others to count the fearful cost of its pursuit. It may have been poor psychology in respect of many crimes and criminals, but there was no ambiguity or contradiction of purpose in it. However, with the introduction of imprisonment as a penal sanction serving purposes beyond the merely deterrent, the seeds of a psychological contradiction were planted.

It will be recalled that the "rehabilitative" program of the late nineteenth-century inventors of the prison had three elements. Rehabilitation was to be achieved by removing the offender from his corrupting peers, by allowing him time for reflection and regenerative self-examination, and by giving him the guidance of uplifting religious and moral precepts. The link was created between time and treatment. The more serious the crime, the more time was needed for the criminal's regeneration. The prison would be humanely purposive, achieving at one stroke its deterrent purposes and its curative potential. The contradiction was implicit from the first day. The penitent willingly suffers the pains of penance for the larger good in which he believes; the self-reformative zeal of the prisoner is less frequently apparent.

Let us leap forward nearly two hundred years and consider the matter in an ideal contemporary "rehabilitative" prison. Now the specifics of treatment are vastly enlarged beyond those available in the shallow medicine-box of the Quakers. All the behavioral sciences are pressed to aid: educational training, vocational training, counseling, group therapy, individual therapy, behavior modification, transactional analysis, Alcoholics Anonymous, Synanon, every emanation of the Oxford Group movement, all in a therapeutic milieu, the whole based on psychiatric, psychological, and physiological diagnosis. All "treatments" will be available to all (at least, in this ideal prison they will). Let me therefore consider the inner contradiction of imprisonment, assuming a generous provision of treatment facilities by a community that has set aside its usually parsimonious budgeting of prison programs.

The inner psychological contradiction is the same for the Quakers' prison at Walnut Street, Philadelphia, as for the most advanced Scandinavian treatment institution. The contradiction lies in the corrupting link between time and treatment, which creates a further corrupting link between coercion and cure.

"Rehabilitation," whatever it means and whatever the programs that allegedly give it meaning, must cease to be a purpose of the prison sanction. This does *not* mean that the various developed treatment programs within prisons need to be abandoned; quite the contrary, they need expansion. But it does mean that they must not be seen as *purposive* in the sense that criminals are to be sent to prison *for* treatment. There is a sharp distinction between the purposes of incarceration and the opportunities for the training and assistance of prisoners that may be pursued within those purposes. The system is corrupted when we fail to preserve this distinction and this failure pervades the world's prison programs.

Unwisely we link the time to be served to involvement in, and apparent response to, prison treatment programs. What is launched as an incentive system turns out to be a barrier to the treatment itself. It may be that, setting aside physiological methods of changing people—surgery, drugs, and the steadying effects of the passage of time—rehabilitation can be given only to a volunteer. We do not know how many volunteers we attract to prison programs. What is sadder, they themselves do not know.

If we were confident that those programs are or could be made truly rehabilitative, it is hard to see why we should churlishly restrict them to the convicted offender. Surely some unconvicted persons, adult and juvenile, would equally benefit from, and would be equally worthy of, the state's beneficent though compulsory assistance toward a better life—a life happier for them and for the community. We limit our benevolence to the convicted, since for them justifications beyond the alleged helping purpose exist for coercively intervening in their lives. Even when our prison purposes are indeed both benevolent and rehabilitative, there is no reason to assume that they are so viewed and experienced by the convicted offender. And, with respect to the efficacy of corrections, as distinct from their aspirations, his perspective and his experience are not without significance. He may believe our purpose to be punitive or deterrent or merely incarcerative while he grows older and the fires of violence or criminality die down—and he may well be right. He may see the rest as rhetoric—and he may well be right.

The treatment model whose rejection I am suggesting is beguiling. Diagnose the social danger presented by the criminal. Give the treatment of choice. Observe if it takes. Relate release to cure. The criminal and society will both gain thereby. It would be a great trick if we could do it, certainly if we could do it without abuse of fundamental human rights; but we cannot.

The treatment model I have sketched has had great appeal to thoughtful scholars of the criminal justice system; it is the foundation on which two schools of criminology have been built—the Positivist School, largely of Italian origins, and the School of Social Defense, dominated by Marc Ancel of France. Despite these distinguished auspices, it seems to me clear that the treatment model suffers from two fallacies, one empirical, the other psychological.

First, the empirical defect. Can we predict the likelihood of criminal behavior in the community by observing the prisoner's response to prison training programs? For present purposes it is necessary to telescope shelves of statistical analysis of parole prediction tables and base expectancy rates for different categories of offenders into overly dogmatic propositions that will be more closely considered in the third chapter. What it all comes to is this: Prison behavior is not a predictor of community behavior.

Does this mean that we cannot develop statistical expectancy tables expressing the differential crime risks of different categories of offenders? Not at all. It means only that observation of the behavior of prisoners while in prison is of little assistance in that regard. Their records before they came to prison, the preservation of such family ties as they have or their improvement while they are in prison, the availability of a place to live and a job to do, all these and similar extra-institutional factors are closely related to later avoidance of criminality (Glaser, 1964). As my colleague Hans W. Mattick suggested: "It is hard to train an aviator in a submarine"; it is even harder to predict his flying capacity from observing his submarine behavior!

These dogmatisms need some qualification, but not much. It is true, for example, that the availability of a job on release may itself turn on the development of vocational skills while in the institution, and to that extent there is a link between institutional training and post-institutional avoidance of crime. However, this is a small oasis in the desert of ignorance regarding empirical relationships between treatment programs and the avoidance of crime.

Second, there is the psychological fallacy that corrupts the individual treatment model. The model of medical treatment that underlies the present advocacy of prison training programs is itself flawed. It suffers fundamentally from a belief that psychological change can be coerced. In psychological treatment of abnormal behavior it is widely agreed that conventional psychotherapy, particularly if it is of the psychoanalytic variety, must be voluntarily entered into by the patient if it is to be effective. By contrast, in physical medicine the cooperation of the patient, although desirable, is not always necessary —an antibiotic works on a patient held down for the injection— and "cure" is a substantially different concept. Yet, in penology the analogy with physical medicine has been accepted since the Quakers first prescribed compulsory segregated religious observance and enforced penitence as their principal specifics.

In the result, throughout the world, particularly in the better correctional systems, we take prisoners through reception and diagnostic classification processes and compulsorily place them in such treatment programs as we have available. We tell them what will work for them and sometimes solicit their acceptance of these programs. But their acceptance is fatally compromised by their clear realization that given indefiniteness of release, given parole and other early release discretions held by correctional authorities, their hope of an earlier freedom is inexorably related to their apparent serious involvement in treatment programs. In one sense they hold the key to their prison, but it is a bogus key. They must present a façade of being involved in their own "rehabilitation" and building that façade may preclude the reality of reformative effort.

That oft-bewildered Martian visitor would surely find it extraordinary that we fill our limited prison treatment and training programs with other than volunteers. We compel people to be in them. As a result neither we nor they know whether they genuinely wish to use such retraining for their personal development toward a happier and less criminous life, or whether they merely seek to "con" those who can earlier open the doors to freedom.

We must abandon the model of physical medicine as a guide. Education, vocational training, counseling, and group therapy should continue to be provided but on an entirely voluntary basis. There should be no suggestion that a prisoner's release may be accelerated because of participation in such programs, nor that it might be delayed or postponed because of failure to participate. Nor in reality should these factors have anything to do with the length of sentence served. The approach adopted should be in no way *coercive* but simply *facilitative*. Rehabilitative purposes must become collateral to prison purposes.

The fundamental jurisprudential issue of power must be restated. In 1964 I offered the view that "power over a criminal's life should not be taken in excess of that which would be taken were his reform not considered as one of our purposes" (Morris & Howard, 1964, p. 175). The sentencing judge should never extend a term of imprisonment, or impose a term of imprisonment, on the basis that the offender needs it for his retraining. That is none of the judge's business.

In 1964, that was not an obvious proposition. Indeed, in an otherwise generous review of the book in which that submission was made, Sanford H. Kadish brusquely inquired: "Why should the rehabilitative purpose be subordinated to the deterrent, vindicatory and incapacitative purposes? (Kadish, 1965, p. 908). Such gentle uncertainties have been swept away by the intervening decade. Few now doubt that large abuses of power under the criminal law may well flow from adjusting power over the criminal's life to the presumed necessities of his compelled cure, time without end, bureaucratic benevolence without sensitivity or self-doubt.

If this rejection of the concept of coerced cure be sound, it raises substantial problems for sentencing, for prison programs and for release procedures, to which we will later return. But in the interim at least one qualification to the elimination of coercion from corrections must be noted.

It is plainly true that people often do not want what they need. It is easy to reject education or vocational training or participation in group therapy if you do not know what it is; indeed, frequently the less you know the easier it is to reject. It is, therefore, not corruptive of a treatment program, nor an improper link between treatment and release, to compel the prisoner to participate in an educational or vocational or psychological training program up to the point where he knows what it is about. In many parts of the world I have seen a sulky and reluctant participant in a group therapy program, sitting stolid, silent, and resentful in the corner, who a few sessions later has been captured by the spirit of the enterprise and has become an involved, vocal, and apparently appreciative participant. Crisis intervention to compel people at least to take stock of alternative avenues of self-development does not debase a treatment program. But I strenuously affirm that the prisoner must be given the unfettered opportunity—and that means an unsanctioned opportunity, deprived of no prison privileges and his release in no way deferred—to decide after a brief compulsory observation of a treatment program that he wants no part of it. For the sake of both those who are participants and those who are running such programs, the prisoner must be freely allowed to reject them.

Why should such stress be placed on the prisoner's right to reject a training program, free of sanction in terms of the duration or conditions of his imprisonment? After all, in most of our dealings out of prison, most of our efforts at advancement or self-development, coercive pressures bear on us. Law students and law teachers alike can hardly be regarded as entirely uncoerced in the classroom. There are pressures on me to write this, I cannot regret them; and on you to read it, and I cannot altogether regret *them*. Few decisions are uncomplicated by the desire to please others, to fulfill obligations, to achieve place or profit; why should the prisoner be so protected from sanctions and incentives to participate in programs which are for his own good as well as ours?

The point has appeal but it underestimates the overwhelming force of the imprisoning power, the isolation, the helplessness, the subservience, of the prisoner. The lawyer is accustomed to drawing a threshold, even an arbitrary threshold, at some point on a continuum. On the continuum of coercion from unfettered and anonymous freedom to physical compulsion, the line of commitment to a prison by order of a criminal court is of such dramatic force and of such labeling consequence that it is a rational line to draw. Operationally, if the prison is to be set free to provide rehabilitative retraining for its inmates, it is a necessary line to draw.

The total institution has such massive impact on its charges, its authority is so annihilative of free choice, that it is essential for us to protect, so far as we can for his sake and for ours, the prisoner's freedom not to be in any treatment programs. We may properly try to persuade him to participate, to lure or cajole him, to tell him of the advantages to him and to us of his participation; but if we are to be free to pursue such persuasions we must guarantee that he will not suffer in prison time or prison conditions from rejecting our advice.

Important consequences would flow from thus exorcising coercion from rehabilitation. The hypocrisy of rehabilitation as a purpose of imprisonment being set aside, the prison culture could both abandon the pretense of rehabilitative purposes for many prisoners and accept retraining objectives for some. It becomes practicable to achieve a better balance within prisons between industrial, recreational, and cultural programs, on the one hand, and educational and behavior-changing programs on the other. Not everything has to wear the mask of rehabilitation, and yet the fact can be addressed that prisons do contain a disproportionate number of the undereducated, vocationally handicapped, and psychologically disturbed. Let me develop these twin themes.

The Abandonment of "The Noble Lie"

Probably the majority of prisoners, like the majority outside the walls, are content to accept themselves as they are and are not anxious to engage in other than recreational and self-indulgent activities outside their working obligations. Though it is certainly true that the prison embraces a disproportionately high incidence of social, psychological, environmental, and physiological casualties, it is also true that character and behavior retraining programs are irrelevant to many prisoners. What would Jimmy Hoffa discuss with his caseworker, in or out of prison, relevant to Hoffa's psyche or the manipulation of power within a union? A discussion between Spiro Agnew and his probation officer, had any unfortunate been appointed to that task, is even more mind boggling. White collar criminals generally are best left to do their prison time without suggestion of their retraining or reform. And, in fact, this is true of very many prisoners no matter what their crime has been. Most murderers are certainly not fit subjects for reform, and it is a mistake to assume that many types of criminal behavior are not rationally (if unwisely) selected by criminals in the light of the social realities of their lives. For these prisoners, if there is reform, it lies in the prison itself, in the steadying processes of aging, in rational decisions that would please even Cesare Beccaria, and we have no need to pretend to overarching reformative purposes here. Many prisoners do decide not to return to crime and adhere as well as the rest of us to such decisions.

The denial that reform of the criminal is a justification for imprisonment has an unexpected tactical disadvantage that merits mention.

The prison should, were the world not full of paradox, be a very paradigm of the rule of law. Until recent years it was instead a hidden land of uncontrolled discretion, the preserve of individual power immune from legal process. As one court phrased it, the prisoner "is for the time being the slave of the State" (*Ruffin v. Commonwealth*, 62 V. [21 Gratt.] 790, 796 [1871]). The courts would look to the legality of the sentence, not to the legality of the conditions of imprisonment. But in the past five years the "hands-off" doctrine has been abrogated and there has been a flood of prisoners' rights litigation. Some prisoners' grievances, some complaints of conditions conflicting with either the Eighth Amendment's proscription of cruel and unusual punishments or the Civil Rights Act's protections of constitutional rights, have been redressed. The impact of this breaching of the prison walls by legal process has been substantial if slow; new professional interests have been focused on penal institutions and, as a result, at least minimum humanities in prisons are better protected and the larger brutalities reduced.

This process of increased judicial control of prison conditions has been eased by what David Rothman called, in this context, "the noble lie" that prisons serve rehabilitative purposes. "Clearly, the rehabilitative ideal has assisted the courts in extending prisoners' rights. While judges have not based their decisions on a right to rehabilitation, they have used the concept to strengthen other kinds of supporting arrangements" (Rothman, 1973, p. 22). Rothman sees danger in this use of "the noble lie," quite apart from its tactical efficacy. "The most serious problem is that the concept of rehabilitation simply legitimates too much. The dangerous uses to which it can be put are already apparent in several court opinions, particularly those in which the judiciary has approved of indeterminate sentences. . . . Moreover, it is the rehabilitation concept that provides a backdrop for the unusual problems we are about to confront on the issues of chemotherapy and psychosurgery. . . . This is not the right time to expand the sanctioning power of rehabilitation" (ibid., p. 24).

If the principles I offer do indeed free the rehabilitative ideal, and properly define its legitimate role, there is no need for "the noble lie" and less danger of expanding the punitive power of the state for curative purposes. The distinction between punishment for rehabilitation and the facilitation of rehabilitative efforts during punishments otherwise justified is a distinction that would be congenial to the judicial mind and would not inhibit effective civil rights and Eighth Amendment litigation of prisoners' grievances. It would be a movement from "the noble lie" to modest truth, properly defining the role of rehabilitative effort within penal institutions, a role that should not be curtailed by cruel and unseemly living conditions, and therefore quite properly adduced to buttress legitimate complaints about inhumane conditions.

What of the other disadvantages Rothman sees in adherence to the rehabilitative ideal? Here he joins Aldous Huxley, David Karp, George Orwell, and Anthony Burgess in foreseeing dangers to liberty in techniques of behavior modification. In 1938, Bertrand Russell put the point well in *Power*: "In former days, men sold themselves to the Devil to acquire magical powers. Nowadays they acquire these powers from science, and find themselves compelled to become devils." The dangers are real. Nevertheless, I submit that the prohibition I have recommended on all efforts at coercive curing under the penal power of the state could be an effective shield against these dangers. But the issue is difficult and demands closer analysis.

The Limits of Prison Treatments, or
"The Ludovico Technique"

Finally, on the value of divorcing coercion from cure let us consider the Ludovico Technique, taking Anthony Burgess's hypothetical aversive conditioning experiment in *A Clockwork Orange* as an illustrative case. You will remember little Alex in Staja 84F, serving his fourteen years as 6655321, speaking to the prison charlie and asking about the new treatment "that gets you out of prison in no time at all and makes sure that you never get back in again." The prison charlie, unresponsive to the inner concerns of little Alex, doubted that the Ludovico Technique, physiologically relating nausea and vomiting to the subject's involvement in violence, "can really make a man good. Goodness comes from within, 6655321. Goodness is something chosen. When a man cannot choose he ceases to be a man." You will further recall that little Alex would have none of the charlie's shilarny but instead promptly signed all available consent and waiver forms, accepting a concentrated fortnight's aversive conditioning in lieu of at least three more years of the brutal bully warders and the vonny leering-like criminals of Staja 84F.

Should aversive conditioning be used in prisons? It merits mention, though carrying analysis no further, that there is at present increasing use of behavioral modification techniques, including aversive conditioning, in prisons and reformatories in this country. For criminal behavior related to addiction to drugs and alcohol, sexual proclivities classed as abnormal, and compulsive gambling there is widespread experimentation with emetics and electric shocks—what the prisoners call "Edison Medicine"—timed to relate to the undesired behavior. And these physiological jolts are given to "volunteers."

Can a prisoner genuinely volunteer for such treatments? Can his consent be withdrawn? What is the proper limit of coercive curing here? The example of little Alex and the Ludovico Technique, putting aside the question of its efficacy which we shall assume, excellently poses the problem.

Let us assume that of one hundred volunteers—people uninvolved with the criminal law but troubled deeply by their

proclivity to violence and freely seeking help in its control—
who viddyed Dr. Brodsky's and Dr. Branom's horrorshow
sinny after the well-timed nausea inducing injections had been
given, the treatment continuing for two weeks, eighty would
over the next two years respond with immediate nausea to any
involvement in a crime of physical violence. The conditioned
response would then attenuate unless it were reinforced, but
would continue substantially to reduce violence in the treated
group. Within the principles so far recommended, may this
treatment be given to little Alex?

The first level of answer is easy; later it grows more complex.
If we are considering volunteers for the Ludovico Treatment
we cannot make the Clockwork Orange bargain. Release and
voluntary treatment cannot be linked. And little Alex simply
would not volunteer absent the promise of prompt release. But
if we divorce all treatments from release, and provide other
means to ensure the prisoner's freedom of decision, such as
prisoner peer group review of the validity of consents to any
treatments (Morris and Mills, 1974) as well as professional
review of the propriety of the more heroic invasions of the
psyche, there would seem no reason why any treatments available in the community should not also be available to the
freely consenting prisoner. It is important critically to test,
carefully to ensure, the uncoerced nature of his consent, but
beyond that the same freedom to be involved in available
treatment modalities should be extended to the prisoner as to
the free citizen—again, for his sake and for ours.

Such successes as are currently achieved in aversive conditioning programs seem to be found particularly in situations
where the subjects of the treatments are profoundly anxious to
change the patterns of their lives—troubled transvestites and
homosexuals, anxious alcoholics, burnt-out drug addicts, and
paid-out gamblers. Again, efficacy and justice combine to favor
volunteering for behavioral modification programs over coerc-
ing prisoners to be involved. Nevertheless, the question of why
prisoners should not be coerced into any program, even the
Ludovico Technique and what it symbolizes of effective aversive
conditioning, psychosurgery, chemotherapy, and other imposed
means of changing behavior, cannot be avoided. It is addressed
at the end of the third chapter. In the meantime one further

suggested qualification must be mentioned to my submission that the prisoner should be free to volunteer for any available retraining or treatment program.

In the *Ohio State Law Forum* Lectures for 1974, Robert Burt discusses the problem of consent to psychosurgery, to the deep implantation of electrodes into the amygdala of a violent patient for diagnostic purposes, and, if necessary, the subsequent destruction or excision of brain cells. He argues that "experimental psychosurgery should not be permitted for involuntarily confined persons, even if these persons consent to the operation" (Burt, 1974, p. 1). He is not referring to any qualified consent; he means an adequately protected, professionally examined, legally reviewable consent. His point is that, if there is substantial risk of injury or personality change, the imprisoned and the inmates of a mental hospital should not be permitted to volunteer for experimental treatments not applied to those at liberty.

Professor Burt's argument is attractive and subtle. It turns on the likelihood of misuse of these techniques if they are tested on prisoners or on inmates of mental hospitals, no matter what care is taken to protect their freedom to consent or to reject such treatments. The prisoner may have a valid interest in running the fully disclosed experimental risk, but the community has an overwhelming interest, so Professor Burt argues, in denying him that opportunity.

I find myself unpersuaded by Professor Burt's analysis by which high-risk experimental treatments must be denied to prisoners. It provides such a transient shield. A few behavioral modification programs in the community, a few hormonal treatments, a few psychosurgical interventions, and the protection that stems from the "experimental" label will be removed. I adhere to the view that it is possible to protect the inmate's freedom to consent or not; that we must be highly skeptical of consent in captivity, particularly to any risky and not well-established procedures; but there seems little value in arbitrarily excluding all prisoners from any treatment, experimental or not. Like free citizens they may consent, under precisely circumscribed conditions (Morris and Mills, 1974) to any medical, psychological, psychiatric, and neurosurgical interventions which are professionally indicated; their protection must be more adequate than that surrounding the free citizen's consent, since they are more vulnerable. It is better directly to confront the potentialities of abuse of power over prisoners than to rely on the temporary exclusion of prisoners from "experimental" programs.

Liberating the Rehabilitative Ideal

Exorcise coercion from treatment programs in prison, let all in such programs be volunteers, leave everything else as is—is that all there is to it? Would it were that easy. Penal reform is more complex. The prison today is inherently coercive in all its aspects. A movement from coerced change to the facilitation of self-change will require the design both of a substantially new model of the prison and of a substantially different system of criminal justice.

It is important to be clear why the rehabilitative ideal is not acceptable as a purpose of punishment. Its corrupting effects on prison programs have been noted, the empirical and psychological fallacies on which it relies have been suggested, but it is necessary to push further into the reasons for rejecting that ideal. Is the point that human behavior is immutable, unchangeable, and that therefore the individualized treatment model should be rejected? Certainly not. After all, if we are sufficiently ruthless in the matter, we *can* coercively cure criminals. The risk of repetition of behavior troublesome to any society by any member of that society can be terminated by capital punishment, by banishment, or by protracted imprisonment. Nor need that imprisonment be for life; aging cures all but the most exceptional proclivities to violent crime. The rejection of that model of treatment as a part of crime control flows not from lack of power or competence to influence the criminal's behavior but from historical evidence about the misuse of power and from more fundamental views of the nature of man and his rights to freedom. These properly limit the power that we wish to accord the state over the individual. We do not suspect, we know, that such powers tend to be abused. So, not even the most perfervid "law and order" sentiment now advocates life imprisonment without benefit of plea bargaining, the modern benefit of clergy, for unarmed housebreakers.

Moreover, we do not reject the rehabilitative ideal, "the individualized treatment model," because human behavior cannot be changed by the actor in collaboration with others assisting him in that change. This is precisely how most effective education is achieved. Nor does this apply only to learning facts or learning techniques or skills. All behavior is in part learned (except certain twitchings of the autonomic nervous system). The milieu is usually of determinative influence, as often are other individuals. I observe that when those among the graduate students of criminology with whom I am in contact who reject the individualized treatment model themselves get into any personal difficulties—and such events are not all that rare—they discuss these matters at sometimes wearisome length with me or with their analysts and manage gradually, partly as a result, to modify their behavior. For themselves, at least, they seem to believe in the individualized treatment model. No, there is nothing at all wrong with the model; the fallacy lies in the reliance on its coercive application outside the proper constraints of a due respect for human rights. So the task is to liberate the individualized treatment model, within the prison setting, for those who for reasons other than treatment are incarcerated. This is the first principle relevant to the new model of imprisonment which I hope to assemble into the rudiments of a working model. I have tried to encapsulate it, in a somewhat pretentious phrase, as *the substitution of facilitated change for coerced cure.* As we saw, there is general agreement on this recommendation in several recent critical studies of the prison, though how such a principle is to be implemented behind the existing walls has been insufficiently explained.

The next principle can also be briefly stated though it will require and will receive extended exegesis in the second chapter: *the substitution of graduated testing of fitness for freedom for parole predictions of suitability for release.* If that sounds somewhat cryptic, I apologize. But there is no reason why social science propositions should always be simple. My obligation is to achieve ultimate clarity, not necessarily to provide instant enlightenment—though it would be pleasant if I could. At all events, these two principles will suffice for a new design of imprisonment and a liberation of the rehabilitative ideal. The application of these two principles to sentencing, classification, prison regimes, parole, and release procedures will, however, require further elaboration.

2

Rehabilitating
the "Rehabilitative Ideal"

The task of defining rational principles for the future of imprisonment is frequently interrupted by denials of the possibility of planning for a humane, parsimonious, just, and socially effective imprisonment. Some of these denials come from thoughtful critics and are not lightly to be dismissed. They argue that even such an effort as mine to liberate the "individual treatment model," to strip it of its coercive, hypocritical, and corruptive elements ought not to be pursued.

Your new model of imprisonment will raise false hopes, they say. It will lead the public to think crime is an emanation of something within the criminal's cranium which can be cut out, doped out, talked out. You will further stigmatize the prisoner. If you make prisons better, less brutal, less obvious circles of hell, more criminals will be sent there. Whatever you build will be filled and what exists will not be emptied. If you want to give new opportunities for self-development to people, to take advantage of them uncoerced, why pick prisoners, why not the poor, the unemployed, the disenfranchised mass in our urban ghettos? Or even better, why not select the victims of crime for this helpful social patronage? No, you pick prisoners because

social policy if it can be done without countervailing disadvantages.

In the first chapter I undertook to limit myself to two principles on which to build a new model of imprisonment. The first was the substitution of facilitated change for coerced cure, and I dwelt at length on the liberating effect of such a principle on prison programs. The second principle strikes deep into the relationship between time and prison programs, and must now be confronted: for parole predictions of suitability for release we must substitute earlier graduated testing of the prisoner's fitness for increased increments of freedom. Let me try to make clear the implications of that proposition.

Predicting and Paroling

Parole boards purport to predict the likelihood of the prisoner's future criminality and to fix his release date partly in relation to that prediction. Understandably, they are particularly concerned by the risk of criminal behavior during the parole period.

A complex of difficulties inheres in this process which is a major impediment to rational prison reform; the more indefinite or indeterminate the sentence imposed, the more intractable is this obstacle to the definition of a new model of imprisonment. As a prelude to considering a major refashioning of the work of parole boards, we must ask what is involved in these predictions of behavior on parole, and how reliable they are.

There are three types of predictions of human behavior: anamnestic, categoric, and intuitive. Let me offer examples of each from criminal behavior, though the analysis is applicable to all behavior. An *anamnestic prediction* is based on observation of the other person's behavior in past identical or similar situations. A prototypical example of an anamnestic prediction of criminal behavior might be based on your observation of that redheaded young man who works in the steel mills stepping through the tavern door one hot payday evening. Over the past year or two he has been involved in a series of tavern fights when alcoholically well lubricated. You make an anamnestic prediction that your friend may have need for lawyer-like or doctor-like services that evening. Unhappily, much of all our lives consists of the repeated manifestation of established patterns of behavior. It takes no close observer of the human condition to see the periodicities and regularities of behavior in the lives of others, or even of ourselves in our more clearsighted moments. Criminal careers, like other careers, have patterns superimposed on the biologic sweep of human life. So, an anamnestic prediction is: the young man behaved in a criminal fashion in a similar situation in the recent past; he has often done so; he is now entering the situation again; he is not unlikely to be involved in crime in the near future.

The second predictive method is statistical or *categoric*. Past experience has led me to the view that on hot Friday nights redheaded people who drink, who have a record of violence, who are between the ages of eighteen and thirty-five, are likely to be involved in crimes of violence. I predict this man's violence, therefore, since he appears to be one of a group who in the past have demonstrated their propensity to violence. This is the reasoning underlying life-expectancy tables, mortality and morbidity tables relevant to surgical and medical interventions, parole prediction tables, sexual psychopath laws, and the disturbed dangerous offender provisions of the Model Penal Code, the Model Sentencing Act, and the numerous state codes they have inspired. Errors of prediction will usually be more frequent in categoric predictions than in anamnestic predictions. Also, categoric predictions are more ambitious since in many cases they aim to predict not only mere *repetition* of the past behavior, but its *escalation* to more serious crime. Thus, the sexual psychopath laws impose extended prison terms on those guilty of minor sexual peccadillos—peepers and flashers, voyeurs and indecent exposers—on the psychologically absurd ground that they are likely to proceed to more heroic or brutal sexual crimes.

Finally, prediction may be merely *intuitive*. Things are going well today; I will take a risk on him. Intuitive prediction reflects a widespread penchant for gambling; it frequently involves an inability to conceptualize or verbalize the logic of anamnestic and categoric predictions. Although we all indulge in it much of the time, intuitive prediction is rather like a numbers game and is unlikely to be more accurate than random chance, despite experiments in extrasensory perception.

Analytically there may be little difference between anamnestic and categoric predictions. All that is being argued about, so some have suggested, is the size of the group to whom the particular person's future behavior is to be related. It is a valid point analytically, but unhelpful in practice. Insofar as anamnestic predictions are related to the close observation of the past behavior of the person under consideration, different techniques for acquiring knowledge upon which to predict are employed. We do not use the experience tables and base expectancy tables that shape the categoric predictions of the better informed parole boards and those whose insurance business depends upon accurate predictions of mortality and morbidity.

Nevertheless, it is certainly true that as clinical study of the individual is pursued there is gradual movement along a predictive spectrum from categoric toward the individual anamnestic prediction. The increasingly precise diagnostic and prescriptive processes in the clinical treatment of the serious physical pathologies are examples of this movement.

There is another distinction between anamnestic and categoric predictions that relates particularly to parole processes. An anamnestic prediction is plainly more explicable to the person under consideration than a categoric prediction. He will more readily accept the fact that the established pattern of his own past behavior has led to the assumption of more punitive power over him than he will accept being treated more severely because of his similarity to an imprecisely defined group of people, some of whom seem to have behaved in a like manner in the past.

To define these three types of predictions separately is, of course, to oversimplify analysis of predictive processes since most predictions of human behavior are based on varying composites of all three. Nevertheless, their artificial isolation is essential if we are to address responsibly the question of the parole board's power based on prediction. Let me put my position concisely and then try to defend it.

Setting aside loss of good time for disciplinary offenses in prison, I submit that it is an abuse of power to extend the duration of an accused person's imprisonment on the basis of predictions of his future criminal behavior, while on parole or thereafter. The parole discretion as it is at present exercised is in all instances an exercise in injustice. Here too, power under the criminal law should be taken only in relation to and limited by proved past criminality, with this qualification—*anamnestic predictions of future behavior may properly be related to the conditions of parole (ceteris paribus, of probation).*

In the third chapter I shall mount as forceful attack as I can on the prediction of dangerousness as a justification for imposing a prison term on an offender who would not be imprisoned absent such a prediction. Everything I offer there is relevant to the present submission. But by way of an introductory point for those who have confidence in parole predictions let me indicate how the matter now stands—empirically.

Two recent studies from the California Department of Corrections research group by Dr. Wenk and his associates (Wenk, 1972) should give pause to any member of a parole board who has confidence in his capacities as a seer of future violent crime. The effort by this skilled research group to develop a "violence prediction scale" for use in parole decisions resulted in 86 percent of those identified as potentially dangerous failing to commit a violent act (more accurately, to be detected in a violent act) while on parole. A parallel effort to predict Youth Authority wards as likely to be violent on parole led to no better predictor than a history of actual violence, and that produced a 95 percent overprediction of violence.

Parole: From Predicting to Testing

Involved in our present sentencing, imprisoning, and paroling theories and practices is the belief not only that human behavior is coercively changeable, within the means properly at our disposal, but also that future criminal behavior by an individual under our control can be predicted by diagnosing his problems and observing his reactions to our treatment. Thus, not only do pre-sentence reports frequently include propositions about the convicted person's likely dangerousness, but also, when reasons are occasionally given by judges for sentences imposed, judicial borrowings from Nostradamus are to be found. And, of course, much of the theory of parole is based on this belief that a likely relationship exists between the prisoner's response to prison and prison treatment programs and his behavior on parole and thereafter. Training for freedom in a situation of captivity is on its face not the easiest of tasks; predicting fitness for freedom from behavior behind bars is even more difficult. Yet that is the trick parole boards are expected, so the theory goes, to achieve.

Let me be plain. I do not argue that parole decision making should be more equitable. I do not argue that applicants for parole should have their cases thoughtfully and carefully considered, or that parole revocation procedures should responsibly incorporate constitutional due process protections, or that parole boards should "be taken out of politics," whatever that means. All these are obviously desirable but they leave the fundamental flaw in the parole process untouched. My assertion is simpler. The link between release on parole and involvement in prison programs must be broken. The best and fairest way to do this is to determine the parole date early. If parole is to be retained, and there are practical reasons why it is likely to be, then the date of the prisoner's first release on parole must be settled and disclosed to him within the first few weeks of his imprisonment.

It would be redundant to rehearse my critique of the rehabilitative ideal as the determinant of the prison term. And the relationship between parole and the individualized treatment model that reflects that ideal is equally clear: give the medicine of treatment, allow release on parole when it takes. Protracted empirical analysis has demonstrated, however, that *predictions of avoidance of conviction after release are no more likely to be accurate on the date of release than early in the prison term* (Goldfarb and Singer, 1973, pp. 278–82; Hood and Sparks, 1970, pp. 183–92). Neither the prisoner's avoidance of prison disciplinary offenses nor his involvement in prison training programs is correlated with later successful completion of parole or with later avoidance of a criminal conviction. Put another way: thirty years of careful compilation of base expectancy rates for parole revocation risk and later conviction risk reveal that only three possible changes in the life of the prisoner during his incarceration are correlated with his later conformity to the conditions of his parole and with his avoidance of conviction for crime after his release—the availability of a family or other supportive social group for him to join on release; the availability of a reasonably supportive job; and the process and duration of aging itself. All three are largely extrinsic to the treatment aspects of prison programs.

Getting a job and preserving or creating social relationships are exactly what prison most interferes with; although time for aging it does provide. We cage men, it is clear, not to treat them; indeed, the caging is likely to preclude self-change toward social conformity; we confine for other reasons. We delude ourselves in thinking that we possess predictive capacities derived from observation of the prisoner's success in prison programs and the time-treatment link we forge on this delusion effectively inhibits the prisoner's relating appropriately to those programs.

On the other hand, if the legislature retains minimum-maximum sentencing, we are wise to determine the parole release date in relation to our knowledge of the risk of serious crime after release by that prisoner. But this can be done early in the prison term as well as later; nothing relevant to the assessment of the risk changes except the prisoner's preservation or formation of social ties or his obtaining a job to go to upon release, and these are matters best handled by a furlough program, by work release, by pre-release opportunities for job finding, by our intelligent support of him in his efforts to create these social and vocational ties. They are certainly better ascertained by testing than by predicting.

Does this criticism of the parole decision lead inexorably to fixed sentencing, as it led the Quakers in *Struggle for Justice,* and to fixed release dates? I think not. I think it is perfectly practicable to keep what is good within the individualized treatment model and to develop techniques of graduated testing of fitness for release as a substitute for our present faulty and fraudulent parole predictions of such fitness. I join the critics in their attack on present paroling arrangements, but two important political points need to be made. They lead me to reject the recommendation in *Struggle for Justice* for fixed, nondiscretionary, and nonparolable periods of incarceration.

Parole has important latent functions that, together with the inertia of social systems, will long preserve the parole process. In addition, the politics of penal reform strongly favor reform recommendations that make use of existing personnel. At its lowest this second point could be regarded as a "jobs for the boys" argument; but it is more than this and incorporates a suggestion that there is often serious opportunity for social advance when one can take two institutional problems and solve them together, rather than flounder with them separately. The two problems to be conjoined inhere in the work of the parole board and of the reception and classification center.

The latent functions of parole, allowing for a sharing of the difficult sentencing discretion between judge and parole board and allowing for the determination of the period to be served at a time removed from the emotional intensity of a criminal trial, will be discussed later when the relationship between judge and parole board in sentencing is considered. All that need be said here as a preamble to the political point I am trying to make is that parole boards are in all states given some power of determining the time to be served by most convicted felons and that there is evidence indicating that of offenders with similar prior records who have been imprisoned for the same offense, ["those . . . who serve the longest terms in prison tend to do less favorably on parole than those who serve the shortest terms before first release" (Gottfredson et al., 1973, p. 25).

The blunt fact is that to get from here to there in penal reform requires a close sensitivity to political issues. It is a mistake for the penal reformer to delude himself into believing in the automatic implementation of sound principles once stated and demonstrated. By and large, the public is uninterested in prison matters, except morbidly at times of riots (particularly if there can be found some sexual overtones to the rioters' behavior). It is a parallel delusion to believe that politicians will long maintain a serious concern for correctional reform. A few will, from genuine social concern, but most are well aware that there are no votes to be gained in penal reform; the lasting banishment of imprisonment, absent escapes and riots, is all that a community expects political leaders to achieve in this sphere.

So, let me suggest that the achievement of penal reform depends on awareness of the politics of change and that change can be facilitated by preserving vocational opportunities for those currently involved in the penal system. Prison, like other social institutions, serves its functionaries. Hence, let me try to put two problems together for the better solution of each. The plan is sketched rather than detailed since to do the latter would require a separate monograph.

Experienced administrators and scholars of the prison system have concluded that the reception and diagnostic centers to which most felons are first sent for what is called "classification" are largely a waste of resources. At most such centers the prisoner spends the first four to six weeks of his incarceration being subjected to physical, psychological, and sociological study and casework analysis; he is then sent on to one of the very few prison placements that are in any event available to him; and the painstaking records prepared in the reception and diagnostic center thereafter rest undisturbed in files, either in that same center or in the institution to which he is assigned. Further, any experienced prison administrator, posted at the front office of the reception and diagnostic center, can, within two days of the prisoner's arrival, predict with high accuracy to which institution he will be sent and which programs will be available to him. Not only can the administrator do this with more than 90 percent accuracy, but he will know which are the 10 percent he is uncertain about. There is, therefore, a steady movement toward the abandonment of such centers for purposes of classification within state prison systems.

The more reflective prison administrators are coming to the view that all reception and diagnostic and classification processes can be truncated to the following: allowing such time as is necessary to decide in the light of the prisoner's record to which of the relatively few available institutions he should be sent; gathering together his records; holding him until convenient transport is available. The prisoner can then be taken to his institution and there inducted into whatever is available for him and expected of him. Of course, a small proportion of prisoners, possibly 10 or 15 percent, will need a more careful diagnostic process. These can be detected, within a day or two, and sent elsewhere or held longer for more protracted, traditional psychological and sociological assessment. In other words, instead of subjecting all prisoners to a lengthy and largely meaningless process, having no relation to prison conditions or programs, it is preferable to let the majority move on immediately to their institutional placement and retain for more thorough assessment only those few for whom "classification" is necessary and for whom there may be some significant relationship between diagnosis and subsequent "treatment."

Now let us add the problem of the parole decision to these suggested changes in reception and diagnostic processes within correctional systems. Much can be said for retaining existing reception and diagnostic facilities and for using them for prompt determination of the first parole release date and the conditions of parole based on anamnestic predictions of behavior. This would be an economy of resources, providing for a single determined effort to acquire and to apply the greatest available knowledge about the accused. It would allow for fixing actual parole release dates somewhat removed from the searchlight of public attention which occasionally focuses on the criminal trial. It would, I submit, keep all that is of value in existing parole processes. Beyond that, the parole date having been set, the prisoner and the prison authorities could turn their attention to arranging an educational, training, or treatment program relating available services to the prisoner's felt needs. It would preserve all that is valuable in our present reception-diagnostic and parole systems and at a stroke eliminate much that is hypocritical, superfluous, and counterproductive.

Such early determinations of the date of first parole would be conditional in the sense that the prisoner's breach of institutional discipline might, upon due process proof of his disciplinary offense, defer his release date. They might also be conditional on the prisoner's having a job available to go to and some supportive living setting; but for these, other pre-release opportunities for community contacts must be given.

There is an argument that the duration of imprisonment and prison disciplinary offenses should not be linked as I have suggested they might be. It runs: only a criminal court should, in respect of a proved criminal offense for which imprisonment is an authorized punishment, have the power to impose or to prolong a sentence of imprisonment. Disciplinary offenses of less gravity than this, or that are tried by processes less formal than those of a criminal court, should never lead to the prolongation of detention; the prisoner should keep his parole release date unless he is convicted by a court of a crime committed in prison. For disciplinary control the prison authorities should limit themselves to the denial of privileges and to other sanctions authorized by the legislature short of loss of time. If time is at issue, the matter is for a court.

There are, it must be admitted, possibilities of abuse of power in prison disciplinary procedures, particularly when the duration of the prisoner's detention is within the competence of the disciplinary tribunal. These risks are not eliminated by the courts' emerging due process controls of prison tribunals' decisions, though they tend to reduce the danger. On the other hand, our present prisons are places of violence and fear; order and discipline must be maintained for staff and prisoners alike; and this is no easy task. There is much to be said for giving the prison authorities, under proper review, the power to use the deterrent weapon of loss of time as a means of achieving some degree of peace and security.

It is a difficult problem, the heritage of protracted overuse of the mega-prison and of the group and racial conflicts these institutions have fostered. Fortunately, its resolution is not essential to my present thesis, but a useful compromise may be suggested.

At present, in typical prison systems the prisoner has a "good time" allowance, a period taken off both his minimum and maximum release dates, apart from the parole date fixed by the board. That is to say, "good time" makes him parolable earlier and means that he must be released earlier. "Good time" is, of course, subject to reduction for disciplinary offenses. In practice, conviction of a prison disciplinary offense may cost him some "good time" as well as influencing the parole board to defer his release on parole.

Under the system I recommend, if the prison authorities are of the view that they need this weapon of time to maintain discipline, it might well be confined to their control over "good time"—a defined period off every month or year served, as an incentive to avoid disciplinary offenses. If the prison authorities believe that the prisoner's behavior in prison is criminal in itself apart from rules of prison discipline and that it requires larger punishment than is available to them, the matter should be referred for prosecution before a criminal court. Otherwise, the prisoner must retain his early determined parole date.

Setting aside the question of prison offenses, the plan I am recommending can perhaps better be presented by way of an example. Consider a convicted armed robber sentenced to from three to five years. Assume his inflexibly good behavior in prison. Assume that his first parole release date—as such matters are at present calculated—would be in two years. Assume further that when the parole board considers his case at the reception and diagnostic center, two years is fixed as his parole release date, independent of his participation in any prison rehabilitative programs. My view of the matter is that it is unjust, an abuse of human rights, to detain him in prison beyond two years on any predictions of his likely future dangerousness. But there are other paths through the prison walls—apart from the dramatic alternatives of the coffin or the tunnel or the sheets over the wall in the fog. Increasingly prison systems allow offenders to go home, or to whatever their community social setting is, on regular furloughs. Increasingly they arrange day-release programs for prisoners who go out daily to work or to school or to college and return in the evenings and weekends to the prison. Increasingly, prison systems—federal, state, and local—arrange pre-release hostel placements for prisoners who, prior to their parole dates, are allowed to live in controlled residential settings in the community while they establish vocational and social ties. In other words, it is clear that there are more paths out of our existing prisons prior to release on parole than there are by way of parole or at the termination of sentence less time off for good behavior.

Self-confidence, one's self-image, are of determinative significance in one's behavior. Even if the overwhelming pressures toward criminality in a particular case are to be found in the familial and social adversities the prisoner suffers and in other criminogenic pressures on him, nevertheless his own perception of his relation to those adversities and pressures and to the community at large, if only in the sense of his capacity to manipulate them in his own self-interest, turns on his own belief in his ability to survive without repeated returns to prison. The principle of graduated testing of his ability to adapt to increased increments of freedom thus makes sense for him and for many prisoners.

For our sakes, as well as the convicted prisoner's, we must extend to him increments of increased freedom prior to his release on parole. He must satisfy himself as well as us that he can go out from prison and live for seventy-two hours or so on furlough without a crime and return to prison. Then, he is ready to take the next step—which may be a work- or education-release program or period out to seek employment, or a pre-release hostel placement, and so on. There should be, in effect, a right to a furlough after a prescribed period in prison. Further furloughs and further opportunities for work release and for pre-parole placement in the community will all depend on the prisoner's avoidance of crime during the earliest graduated test periods and, though I regret complicating the matter, they will depend also on his conformity to any other appropriate conditions upon his outside behavior that we might impose.

Some commentators have suggested that it is unwise to impose probation and parole conditions beyond the requirement to observe the dictates of the criminal law that is in any event imposed on all of us, convicted and unconvicted alike, without need for special prescription. I do not share this view. Rather, I see a limited but important role for the imposition of behavioral conditions anamnestically related to the offender's past criminality. The point is of importance to this effort to rehabilitate the rehabilitative idea; it is central both to rational sentencing and to a rational criminal justice system.

Conditions of probation and parole, other than an obligation to report or to be available for supervision or not to leave a defined geographic area, should never be imposed by judge or parole board unless they are closely and directly related to the crime for which sentence is being imposed or which brought to prison the criminal now being paroled. Only if the offender is free *not* to accept the support and assistance of the probation officer or parole officer can he be free to accept such assistance and therefore, taking the mass of offenders, for us to gain thereby. Here, too, rehabilitative purposes can be achieved only if they are cut free of coercion. And further, only if there is a clearer distinction between the probation or parole officer's supervisory (police) role and his supportive (social welfare) role can he be free to relate usefully to such offenders as may gain from his assistance to them.

Note, however, an important exception to that principle. Conditional limitations on freedom—residential, educational, vocational, family relational, or related to available community-based treatment programs—may be justified if a close anamnestic relationship is established on the record (thus subject to appropriate appeals or judicial control of administrative discretion) between the crimes of which the offender was convicted and the aspects of his behavior to be limited by the condition.

An example may assist. Assume our armed robber committed his past crimes as sequels to alcoholic benders—a not uncommon sequence. It would seem entirely appropriate to make it a condition of his parole that he should not consume alcohol for the duration of the parole term. Such a condition is justified for our benefit, but its relationship to his past behavioral history can and should be made apparent to him, which is a clear advantage of anamnestic predictions over categoric predictions.

In sum, then, restructuring reception-diagnostic and paroling systems and limiting conditions of parole as I have suggested will minimize the corruptive link between time and treatment which inhibits such potential for good as exists in our present prison training and parolee assistance programs and will allow room for an individual treatment model within the prison system without abuse of power.

Parole: The Contract System

The idea of early fixing of the parole date is not farfetched. It has been done and is currently being tested. F. Lovell Bixby, a creative force in American corrections who served on the first Adult Authority in California, tells me that he and his two colleagues, Lewis Drucker and Walter Gordon, appointed pursuant to the 1944 Californian statute inaugurating that experiment with the indeterminate sentence, made it a general practice to advise the prisoner of his parole date when they first interviewed him, about six months after admission. In the interim, the reception and classification work would have been completed. The purposes were, in Bixby's words, "to give the man some notion of what to expect . . . [and] to render him eligible for minimum security camp early in the sentence." Lovell Bixby brought these ideas from New Jersey, where they had been applied to young offenders in that state's reformatories. These practices ceased in New Jersey and California, not because of any dissatisfaction with their influence on the offenders to whom they were applied or on institutional training programs, but for bureaucratic reasons.

There is also contemporary advocacy of and experimentation with the idea of early settlement of the parole date.

In December 1972, the Forty-second American Assembly met in Arden House, New York, and drafted a series of recommendations entitled "Prisoners in America." Like other contemporary critics of the American criminal justice system, they argued that "it is fruitless to cling to the rehabilitative ideal," but they added, "Nevertheless we do not advocate locking up the offender and throwing away the key. Although coercion has failed for the most part, it does not necessarily follow that voluntary programs are doomed to the same fate. Consequently every prison has the obligation to provide opportunities for prisoners who choose to pursue them." So far, I agree, but how is this conjunction of prison and voluntarism to be achieved? "States should experiment," the American Assembly suggested, "with arrangements whereby inmates make written agreements with the parole board and the prison staff to complete a specific program of institutional activities. Release would be automatic upon the inmate's completion of the agreed upon plan" (American Assembly, *Report*, 1973, pp. 5–7).

With the support of the Department of Labor several states— notably Wisconsin, Arizona, and California—have developed Mutual Agreement Programs involving the negotiation of precise, legalistically phrased contracts between the prisoner, the parole board, and the department of prisons, based on a reception, orientation, and evaluation period early in his prison term. Descriptions of these programs exist, but as yet no outcome data are available (American Correctional Association, 1973).

Such plans are an effort to gain the advantages of an uncoerced training program, of fulfilling the American Assembly's principle of voluntarism, without adopting anything like the more far-reaching reforms of the criminal justice system I have suggested. Having a psychological preference for the line of least resistance, I would tend to prefer these ideas of contractual negotiation of prison programs if I thought they had a chance of success; but I do not. Since the reason is one of principle, I must offer it.

The contract negotiated between the prisoner and parole and correctional authorities is an effort to engage him in programs designed for his self-development without the uncertainty of the duration of his imprisonment hanging over his head. It is clearly a step in the right direction, but its defect is obvious. The prisoner can hardly be thought to be in a free negotiating situation when he knows that his involvement in the program, or rather his apparent agreement to involvement, is an important factor in determining how long he will be in prison. Free contracting is not easy in such a situation; there is more than a hint of duress, of *force majeure*. And as time passes, as the prisoner reflects upon this "contractual" relationship, he must see its inner coercive quality. He may not regret the contract; he may agree with the wisdom of what he has done; but he must recognize that the agreement was tainted by the weakness of his bargaining position. The state had a right to detain him, to punish him. It did not have a right to train or treat him against his will and his will was not free in this contract. As the Mafia is reputed to do, the state here made him an offer he could not refuse.

Sentencing and Plea Bargaining

I have reached a point in my submissions where I have offered principles that will preserve what is good in present correctional programs and at the same time allow for the elimination of what is coercive, unjust, and dysfunctional in them. I have, to put no modest turn of phrase on the matter, advanced principles upon which a rational and just prison program might be built. But here I reach a point of interrelationships with other aspects of the criminal justice system that precludes the comforting artificial isolation of the topic of imprisonment that has made possible my so far optimistic analysis. Our present sentencing practices are so arbitrary, discriminatory, and unprincipled that it is *impossible* to build a rational and humane prison system upon them.

This is not the occasion to offer a rounded thesis on sentencing. For present purposes all I need do is to express my enthusiastic support for the broad directions of sentencing reform powerfully urged by Judges Marvin E. Frankel (Frankel, 1973) and Constance Baker Motley (Motley, 1973)—note my particular enthusiasm for Judge Motley's observation that "By punishing the defendant for what he is, rather than for what he has done, some sentencers loosen what may already be a fragile tie between the defendant and society" (ibid., p. 269)—and offer my own ideas on the minimum conditions of a fair sentencing system necessary for the recommendation I am making for the future of imprisonment.

A first helpful insight is to be gained by considering who it is that imposes sentences in our criminal justice system. As we have seen, all our diversionary programs can properly be regarded as sentencing, that is, as the imposition of conditional restrictions upon accused or sometimes convicted persons. But I want to face the narrower issue of the decision as to the appropriate punishment for a convicted offender who has not been diverted from traditional sentencing processes. Let me suggest that at present such sentences are determined in the main by agreements between the prosecutor and the defense counsel. Charge and plea bargaining is our primary sentencing technique. As to the residue, the less than 10 percent of felony charges that go to bench or jury trials, the judge controls the sentence to be imposed in the sense that it is he, guided by whatever presentence advice he cares to take and to a degree by the views of prosecutor and defense counsel, who determines whether the convicted person shall be sent to prison or shall be treated in some other fashion—by fine or by suspended sentence or some form of conditional liberty such as probation. If the judge determines that a prison sentence is appropriate, then the most usual practice in this country is that he will impose a minimum-maximum term, an indefinite or indeterminate sentence, with the boundaries more or less precisely defined, the least defined being in California with its completely indeterminate sentence. It is clear, therefore, that the judge shares his sentencing responsibility with the parole board, who can fix the parole date within the boundaries set by the judge.

Whatever other inequities and inefficiencies may be preserved within our complex sentencing processes, it seems clear that a rational prison program cannot be built upon our present plea bargaining and prison time determining processes.

Let me separate these two issues, dealing first with the relationship between judge and parole board in the determination of the time to be served and later with the challenging problem of sentences imposed in the Moorish market place of our present plea bargaining practices.

Sentencing: Judge and Parole Board

The discussion is based on an assumption that the judge has decided to impose a prison sentence. The modern criminal codes, having their genesis in the work of the American Law Institute's Model Penal Code, tend to reduce the categories of offenses in number and to circumscribe more carefully the exercise of the judicial sentencing discretion. I wish to accept all that as a series of moves in a clearly desirable direction and to consider only the relationship between the judge and the parole board in regard to the duration of time to be served; herein lies, in my view, a substantial barrier to the design of a rational prison system.

Why should the judicial sentencing discretion be shared at all with the parole board? The traditional answer was clear. By observing the prisoner's response to the treatment program, the board could adjust the date of his release to the likelihood of his avoidance of crime in the future. They could both better protect the community and extend clemency to the prisoner based upon his response to the rehabilitative efforts made on his behalf. It was a fine idea having only the defect that it did not work. My earlier attack upon the idea of parole need not be repeated. All that need be offered here is the dogmatic affirmation that some thirty years of careful effort to discover a relationship between prison behavior and later social conformity has proved abortive. The age of the prisoner, the availability to him on release of reasonably remunerative employment and of a supportive domestic environment, are closely related to his later avoidance of crime, but these are not circumstances over which the prisoner by his own efforts while in prison has very much control. There is no need for a judge to share his sentencing power with the parole board in order to relate to these three aspects of the prisoner's post-institutional life.

Yet it would be a superficiality to reject a division of power between judge and parole board simply because the parole board is unable to predict behavior in the community by observing behavior in prison. As we have seen, there are other methods of testing fitness for release—graduated testing programs rather than efforts at prediction. And, more importantly, one latent function of parole must be mentioned. The judge imposes sentence at a time of high emotional response to the facts of the crime. Even within our grossly dilatory system of justice, the sentence follows closely upon the public narration of the criminal events, if not upon the commission of the crime. A parole board, however, may make its decision in what one hopes will be a less punitive social atmosphere. One important latent purpose of probation is to allow a judge to give the appearance of doing something while in fact doing nothing. Similarly, one latent purpose of the division of power between judge and parole board is to give the possibility of some clemency while appearing in the public eye to be imposing a more severe punishment.

Whether overall parole has indeed achieved a reduction of prison time served in America is speculative. In individual cases it has made possible leniencies that were politically impractical at the time of trial, but it is not known whether this has been counterbalanced by the public's and the judge's knowledge of the operation of parole and by his accommodating the sentences he imposes to parole board practices. The tendency of parole boards to overpredict danger and to follow the politically safer path of prolonging incarceration because of exaggerated expectations of criminality on parole (which will be discussed in the next chapter) would lead one to suspect that parole may well have increased total prison time. But reliable data are lacking.

Nevertheless, in the present state of human knowledge a justification of a division of power between judge and parole board in determining the appropriate period of freedom that should be taken from a convicted offender cannot rest upon the assertion that the parole board can predict the offender's later social conformity better than the judge. Of course, the parole system may well be preserved for the future by the inertia of social institutions, the latent effects of the division of sentencing power, and the self-protective efforts of an entrenched bureaucracy. If it is, this at least must be changed if we are to free prison programs for their potential contribution to social welfare: parole boards must determine the date of first parole, subject to the prisoner's good behavior in the institution, early in his prison term. Only thereafter can educational, vocational, psychological, and other training programs offered to the prisoner be accepted voluntarily by him.

Hence, we reach the following first condition of sentencing if there is to be a just and rational prison system. Either the term imposed must be fixed by the judge, or if the term be indeterminate or indefinite and subject to parole, the parole board must determine the date of release in the first few weeks of the prisoner's incarceration and advise him of that date.

Some qualifying comments on this principle are necessary. In whatever way the term of imprisonment is determined, there is necessity for some control of prison behavior by "good time" or by other techniques of relating the term served to the avoidance of serious disciplinary offenses by the prisoner.

There may also be value in preserving some indeterminacy of sentencing by the judge for purposes akin to those we saw could be served by conditions of parole and probation. As yet there are only straws blowing in the wind to support the following suggestion, but the idea perhaps merits consideration: if it is justifiable to allow a convicted offender to be at large in the community subject to behavioral conditions anamnestically related to his crime, and we have suggested earlier that that is a justifiable sentence, then exactly the same thing may be true when a prison term has been imposed. Putting aside for the moment the question of who imposes the sentence, a sentence of the following form has criminological validity within our existing empirical knowledge and is rationally comprehensible to the public and to the convicted criminal as a fair sentence. Let us assume a drunken driver who has injured another. Consider the following sentence: "I sentence you to from one to three years in prison. If you avoid disciplinary offenses while in prison you will be released after you have served one year less time off for good behavior. In the ensuing two years you will be prohibited both from drinking and from driving a motor vehicle. If you do either of these during that period— proved to our satisfaction—you will have to serve a further two years of imprisonment. Your present offense and your prior criminal record justify this combination of prison time and conditional freedom."

It is an exaggerated example, designed to make a point. Such attachments of rational conditions to freedom might well justify what amounts to a two-part sentencing by a judge, one period in prison and the other under defined conditions in the community. A sentence of this sort could as well be given by a parole board if the judge merely imposed a one- to three-year term, leaving the anamnestically related conditions of freedom to be assessed by the parole board.

There are other problems concerning the duration of supervision under conditional liberty after a prison term has been served that raise difficulties both under our present sentencing system and under that which I am advocating, but they can be finessed now as less important than the central point that there must be no relationship whatsoever between time to be served and the treatment program if such programs are to be practicable within the prison setting.

There were two reasons why it was essential to discuss sentencing as a precondition to the shaping of the future of imprisonment. First, the fraudulence of the link between prison program and release date is understood not only by all prisoners but by all working in the prison setting. Some legislators and some of the public may occasionally be deceived by the rhetoric of rehabilitation; prisoners and prison staff rarely are. Second, there is at present such a pervading sense within prison of the injustice of sentencing that any rehabilitative efforts behind the walls are seriously inhibited. In the long run, until sentencing can become principled, until a jurisprudence of sentencing supported by an ample common law and the articulation of criteria of punishment can be phrased and applied, the task of the penal reformer will remain intractable. This leads me to the second relationship that has corrupted the judicial sentencing role, namely, plea bargaining.

Sentencing: Plea Bargaining

On the order of 90 percent of those convicted and sentenced for serious offenses throughout federal and state systems have pleaded guilty. They do this rarely because of any Pauline conversions to virtue on the road to the courthouse. Their guilty pleas are the product of the threat of a larger punishment if they do not plead guilty or, phrased more generously, of uncertainty about what their punishment would be if they risk either bench or jury trial.

The literature on plea bargaining is substantial and rapidly growing (Alschuler, 1968; A.B.A., 1968; A.L.I., 1972; Enker, 1967; Harvard L. Rev., 1970; National Advisory Commission, *Courts*, 1973). The topic merits book-length consideration but it is necessary that at least brief consideration now be given to the relationship between plea bargaining and the prison of the future, since it is in my view impossible to build a humane and just system of imprisonment on the foundation of our present plea bargaining practices.

The inequities and awkward compromises involved in charge and plea bargaining have frequently been discussed; indeed, it is no exaggeration to suggest that the strongest defense of our present plea bargaining practices that is offered is based on expediency and on the reluctance of the community to allocate sufficient resources to the determination of guilt or innocence and to the settlement of the appropriate punishment for guilt. Other than uneasy and unconvincing arguments that these practices provide room for that repentance which properly calls forth mercy and certainly facilitates rehabilitation, I hear no principled argument for charge or plea bargaining. There are, to be sure, principled reasons for pre-trial settlement of criminal charges in many cases, but charge or plea or punishment concessions to purchase such settlements are defended primarily in terms of expediency. Predominantly what is offered by the supporters of plea bargaining are arguments as to its unavoidability in the present circumstances of the courts, particularly the city courts, together with a proliferation of rules of practice and procedure, such as those offered by the American Bar Association Minimum Standards Project or required by federal or state Rules of Court, designed to avoid the grosser injustices and improprieties in plea bargaining. What such reformist efforts seem to amount to is, in the language of diplomacy, the rejection of secret covenants secretly arrived at and the advocacy of open covenants secretly arrived at. The judiciary seems more interested in protecting its trailing robes from the dirt of the market place than in overturning the tables or regulating the market.

Prisoners are, I assure you, amply aware that plea bargaining is another name for sentencing. They are aware that the most effective defense counsel is not the counsel who can adduce the best defense but is rather that counsel who can obtain the best deal. The more experienced in crime the prisoner is, the more he has come to appreciate the negotiative quality of the American criminal justice system. "Get me Agnew's lawyers," they all plead.

At last a national commission, the National Advisory Commission on Criminal Justice Standards and Goals, has recommended the abolition of plea concessions. Their recommendation has been met with outrage by many criminal law practitioners and has almost sunk in the turbulence of prejudiced debate. It has not proved easy to persuade the legal profession, in particular the criminal bar, that the abolition of plea concessions does not mean the abolition of pre-trial settlement of criminal charges. What corrupts is the concession for the plea, not the pre-trial settlement. Useful analogs for reform lie to hand in the pre-trial settlement of civil issues, in certain arbitration practices, and in various European models of pre-trial disposition of criminal charges. In particular, the broad pattern of pre-trial consensual settlement of civil disputes is one that can readily be adapted to criminal law issues without any requirement of concessions for a plea. Again, this issue, like that of the relationship between judge and parole board, merits extended analysis. It suffices for my present task, however, to sketch the bare outline of pre-trial disposition processes which may lead to the imposition of a prison term and which, unlike present plea bargaining, would not preclude the creation of a rational and just prison system.

At present, there are two parties to the plea bargaining: the prosecutor and the defense counsel. Allegedly the defense counsel advises his client with precision of a possible settlement and of the likely sentence which will flow from alternative trial procedures. But, as every practitioner knows, there are many pressures upon defense counsel to narrate those facts inaccurately. For example, some acquaintance with the operation of plea bargaining in the crowded city courts of this country has led me to the conclusion that it is in the interests both of the prosecution and of the defense counsel for the prosecution to "overcharge" the accused. There is then available something by way of charge "concession" for the defense counsel to get for his client and, obviously, the prosecutor's bargaining position is strengthened by overcharging. Likewise, it is in the interests of both counsels to tend to exaggerate the severity of the sentence which might be imposed pursuant to conviction after a bench trial or a jury trial. Again, defense counsel's interests differ from those of his client; again he can more likely win something, if only a lesser sentence than was feared. And obviously, if defense counsel has reasonable expectations of settling a plea, there is substantial pressure on him to exaggerate to his client the risks of bench and jury trial and to overstate the likely disadvantages of not accepting a bargain which counsel thinks wise.

The judge also becomes a mere secondary party, advised by the first two parties of the conclusions of their negotiations, having only a veto power over them, a veto power he can exercise only rarely if the trial system is not to break down. I recognize that in some jurisdictions judges participate to varying degrees in plea bargaining discussions and that there are a few official recommendations that they should do so, but I have stated the general pattern.

So, as a first and obviously essential reform we start with the requirement of the presence of at least four parties for any sound pre-trial dispositive process: judge (clearly not the trial judge, if the matter goes to trial), prosecutor, defense counsel, and accused. Apart from other reasons, the constitutional right to presence at trial can only be given reality if the accused is allowed to attend those aspects of the pre-trial processes that are of significance to him. Now he is present only for the formalities, the signing of the treaty, not its negotiation.

I wish to add a fifth party to these pre-trial dispositions, but before I do so let me suggest one model of pre-trial discussion to be conducted without concessions—and by that I mean without the prosecution's speaking at all as to either the charge to which it would accept a plea of guilty or the sentence it would regard as appropriate—other than in open discussion of these matters at the pre-trial hearing.

A pre-trial hearing should be called by a judicial officer in respect of every criminal charge for which a true bill has been found or an equivalent preliminary hearing process completed. It is important that the pre-trial hearing be called in every case and that no report of such pre-trial discussions should be available in any case to a trial judge if the matter subsequently goes to trial. There must be no record kept of the pre-trial discussions, and no statements made there must be admissible either in examination-in-chief or in cross-examination if the matter goes to trial.* The pre-trial hearing has two purposes. First, if the matter is set down for trial, to lay out a timetable of preliminary motions and trial hearings so that at least we may begin to give reality to the promise of speedy trial. The pre-trial hearing could thus become an inhibitor of "trial by diary," which is the customary technique of manipulating continuances and "burning off" witnesses to the advantage of the more prosperous and privately represented accused and therefore to the detriment of the rest. The second purpose is to explore what might be feasible by way of a settlement of all issues in dispute, acceptable to the state and the accused alike, including questions of compensation of victims, and everything that is now properly relevant to plea bargaining.

Complementary to such a pre-trial dispositional hearing would be a professional ethical prohibition on private consultation between prosecutor and defense counsel regarding any

---

*There is a delicate Fifth Amendment point that merits mention. Neither admissions nor confessions should be required of the accused at the pre-trial conference. There are no effective protections against at least the psychological consequences of such admissions or confessions if the case goes to trial. The silence of the record is not an adequate protection against the fruits of this tainted tree. Hence, it will be necessary to conduct pre-trial discussions on the assumption, made explicit by the judge, that the accused did the prohibited act on which the charge is founded. This does not speak to guilt; there may be *mens rea* issues and justifications of relevance. Nor would the accused have to agree to his having done the act—the assumption is merely the express base for the pre-trial discussion. At any time he has an unfettered right to terminate the discussion and to go to bench or jury trial. Of course, issues of adequacy of proofs would be open for discussion. In sum, the Fifth Amendment problems are real but by no means insuperable.

matters at issue in the pending case, akin to the prohibition on private consultation between judge and counsel concerning pending litigation in which they are both involved. In effect, all charge and plea bargaining would be pursued in the controlled setting—and only there.

It would seem to me that in such a setting everything that is good in our present plea bargaining processes can be retained and much that is evil in them can be eliminated. It is obvious that the accused has an unfettered right to go to trial and to refuse to accept any product of such a pre-trial discussion. Likewise, a veto power must be held by the judge, though for different and distinct reasons. But absent the exercise of either of these two veto powers, a prison sentence based on such a pre-trial discussion and settlement of the issue can hardly be regarded by the prisoner as other than one in which he has been fairly and justly treated. He is potentially liberated from any sense of injustice and set free for whatever involvement in any prison retraining program that is available and in which he wishes to engage himself.

I suggested that there should be a fifth person at the proposed pre-trial hearings. So far, in making these recommendations concerning pre-trial disposition of criminal cases, I have been guided by various existing dispute settlement models; but in recommending a fifth person at these pre-trial hearings I go beyond what has been tested elsewhere and move to the more speculative. The victim should have the opportunity of being present at the pre-trial hearing. This does not mean that he should, like the judge and the accused, have a veto power over any proposed settlement of the issues, but he certainly represents an important interest of the criminal justice system and should be allowed to be heard on the suitability of any pre-trial settlement and on the acceptability of any compensatory arrangements.

With some trepidation I wish to offer a psychological argument in favor of bringing the victim into these proceedings.

At present, victims of crimes are treated extraordinarily shabbily by our criminal justice system. The system appears to serve its functionaries more than the public. Victims are repeatedly interrogated; they make too many trips to pre-trial and trial hearings, at most of which they sit doing nothing, unable to hear the proceedings, forbidden to talk or read, bewildered as to what is going on, wondering whether they are the wrongdoers or not, and reflecting on their lost wages and other costs. States are extremely parsimonious in arranging compensation in respect of injuries to them from crimes of violence. Further, in that criminal proceedings take precedence over civil proceedings, the state processes also tend to sweep away what few resources most criminals have that might be used for compensating the victim civilly for the harm he has suffered. But merely because we treat victims shabbily now does not mean that they should be involved in the pre-trial discussions I have recommended; a more affirmative justification must be offered.

If the criminal process is the taking over by the state of the vengeful instincts of the injured person—buttressed by the recognition that the harm to the victim is also harm to the state—then it would seem, at first blush, that the victim at least has a right to be informed of, and where appropriate involved in, the processes that have led to whatever is the state settlement of the harm that has been done to him. In that respect, one would hardly need to make an affirmative argument; it is a matter of courtesy and respect to the dignity of the individual victim. If his acceptance of any compensatory arrangements is to be introjected into the settlement, as it should be more frequently than it is now, his presence is essential. But I suggested that there were also psychological reasons for the submission I have made.

Let us look at the matter first from the viewpoint of the offender. Self-reform presupposes self-forgiveness. Mercifully time allows most of us this privilege, no matter what happens, but self-forgiveness is very much more swift and practicable when the person we have injured forgives us. These propositions hardly merit exegesis; they are either acceptable to you or they are not; they are deeply ingrained in the world's literature; they are, I submit, the product of all human experience. They do not mean that the victim has any obligation to forgive the person who has wronged him. They simply affirm that, if we hope for change in the wrongdoer, that change will be expedited by his being forgiven by the person he has wronged. A pre-trial settlement in which the victim agrees does give the convicted criminal, in prison or not, an opportunity to begin again if he wants to—and immediately.

Now from the perspective of the victim. Let me take a particularly difficult case, a forcible rape, and suggest that the principles of psychological analysis offered here apply also, though in varying degree, to all other crimes against the person and to all crimes against property. It is in most cases desirable for the psychological health of the victim of the rape that she comes to understand that her aggressor was not just a nameless fear in the night. She too may gain by coming to recognize the larger existential misery of this human encounter. As the rapist must see that the woman was not just a bundle of flesh but was also a wife or mother, so that he can personify his guilt, so it is often desirable for the victim's personal well-being that she should come to see her aggressor as part of the human condition. Again it must be stressed, there is no obligation for the victim either to attend or to participate in such pre-trial disposition. But this opportunity should be afforded to the victim supported by the suggestion that in many cases it is both socially and psychologically sound for her to do so. The argument is, of course, easier to make in respect of the attendance at the pre-trial dispositional hearing by victims of crime less psychologically disturbing than rape.

To try, as the young now advise, to get it all together: there can be no rational future for imprisonment unless present plea bargaining practices, which are the main dispositive technique for sentencing criminals, are rendered principled and orderly, and unless sentences imposed at trial by the judge and thereafter by the parole board are set free from the crippling link between prison program and release date. If these liberations are achieved, then applying principles earlier enunciated, prison may play a rational and functional role in the criminal justice system.

3

The Justification
of Imprisonment

Principles have been offered to guide the future of imprisonment. The next step is to suggest principles to determine who should be in prison. That is the purpose of this chapter, with an added topic of relevance to penal theory: if a prisoner would be a danger if he were at large, why should he be let out?

It may already be suspected that my efforts to rehabilitate the rehabilitative ideal fail to conceal a punitive approach to penology. And so it is. In my view, penal purposes are properly retributive and deterrent. To add reformative purposes to that mix—as a purpose of the sanction as distinct from a collateral aspiration—produces neither clemency nor justice. To add incapacitative purposes is likewise unjust. But argument rather than affirmation will be required.

To cut through the rhetorical foliage that characterizes most jurisprudential discussion of the purposes of punishment, let me try to address, by way of completing this new model of imprisonment, two blunt questions:

Why should a convicted criminal be imprisoned?

Why should we risk future criminality by convicted criminals?

In responding to these two questions, it is my hope to state a philosophy of imprisonment under which that residual sanction of the criminal law can be applied with restraint and humanity until it is no longer needed for social control.

I. WHY SHOULD A CONVICTED CRIMINAL BE IMPRISONED?

As usual, it is necessary to be clear about what is not implied in this question as a prelude to offering an answer to what is. I am not discussing the challenging problems involved in setting the term of imprisonment so that like cases will be treated alike and all treated fairly. The attempt is rather to offer principles which should govern decisions on whether or not a sentence of imprisonment should be imposed. These principles will, with suitable modifications, apply also to the assessment of the appropriate duration of imprisonment by the legislature and by the judge, and to all sentencing decisions as they are later taken by both parole boards and correctional authorities. However, for ease of exposition, the present analysis isolates the issue of *imprisonment vel non*. The objective is to offer principles upon which a jurisprudence may evolve to determine whether the judge should impose a sentence of imprisonment or some lesser sanction. Although these principles apply whenever this issue is addressed—by the legislator, the policeman, the prosecutor, the judge, the parole board member—it will further assist analysis to focus on the judge's decision.

It may also make for clarity of presentation first to state the whole answer *tout court* and then to discuss its details. Three principles to guide the decision to imprison are submitted. Thereafter, three preconditions to the judicial imposition of a sentence of imprisonment are presented. (These latter are conjunctive; all three must be met before imprisonment should be ordered.)

Principles Guiding the Decision to Imprison
  1. Parsimony
     The least restrictive (punitive) sanction necessary to achieve defined social purposes should be imposed.
  2. Dangerousness
     Prediction of future criminality is an unjust basis for

determining that the convicted criminal should be imprisoned.

3. Desert

No sanction should be imposed greater than that which is "deserved" by the last crime, or series of crimes, for which the offender is being sentenced.

Preconditions to Imprisonment

A. Conviction by jury or bench trial or an acceptable plea of guilty to an offense for which imprisonment is legislatively prescribed.

and

B. Imprisonment is the least restrictive (punitive) sanction appropriate in this case because:

either   i) any lesser punishment would depreciate the seriousness of the crime(s) committed,

or   ii) imprisonment of some who have done what this criminal did is necessary to achieve socially justified deterrent purposes, and the punishment of this offender is an appropriate vehicle to that end,

or   iii) other less restrictive sanctions have been frequently or recently applied to this offender.

and

C. Imprisonment is not a punishment which would be seen by current mores as undeserved (excessive) in relation to the last crime or series of crimes.

All this is, no doubt, cryptic and opaque. It may assist if I offer some commentary on the principles suggested to guide the decision to imprison and then draw a sharp contrast between the preconditions to imprisonment submitted here and those adopted in most of the recent criminal codes.

Principles Guiding the Decision to Imprison

1. Parsimony

The first principle recommends parsimony in the use of imprisonment. The least restrictive—least punitive—sanction necessary to achieve defined social purposes should be chosen. This principle is not novel. A presumption in favor of punishment less severe than imprisonment pervades all recent scholarship and most legislative reforms. This principle is utilitarian and humanitarian; its justification is somewhat obvious since any punitive suffering beyond societal need is, in this context, what defines cruelty. An emerging case law and commentary supports this principle (Singer, 1972). It has the strong support of the American Law Institute in its Model Penal Code and of the American Bar Association's Project on Minimum Standards for Criminal Justice. The principle of parsimony infuses the recommendations of the two national crime commissions of the past decade. Its constitutional support is hesitant, but the analogies are clear. Imprisonment, as a sanction for a common cold or for being a narcotic addict, would, we are assured, be unconstitutional (*Robinson v. California*, 370 U.S. 660 [1962]); to put a prisoner involved in a scuffle with another prisoner into maximum security segregation for two years offends the Eighth Amendment's proscription of cruel and unusual punishments (*Fulwood v. Clemmer*, 206 F. Supp. 370 [D.D.C. 1962]); the death penalty would be unconstitutionally pronounced for a rape in which life was neither taken nor endangered (*Ralph v. Warden*, 438 F. 2d 786 [4th Cir. 1971] cert. denied, 408 U.S. 942 [1972]). Further, this principle of parsimony has been expressly accepted by the courts and by legislatures in relation both to the civil commitment of the mentally ill and retarded and to the duration and conditions of their detention (Harvard L. Rev., 1974, pp. 245–53).

A principle similar to that of the least restrictive (punitive) sanction is offered by Goldstein, Freud, and Solnit, in their important study *Beyond the Best Interests of the Child*, as applicable to all issues in which child placement by a court is at stake, expressly including juvenile delinquency matters involving violence where "even if the law were to make society's immediate safety the primary goal, we would argue that within that ambit the least detrimental alternative placement should be selected" (p. 153, n. 11).

The draftsmen of the American Law Institute's Model Penal Code sought to capture this principle of parsimony in imprisonment in the phraseology of that code's main article on sentencing. Section 7.01 is entitled "Criteria for withholding sentence of imprisonment . . ." and the section directs the court to order other punishments unless "imprisonment is necessary for protection of the public." Later state and federal legislative reforms and proposals have followed the path to the least restrictive sanction prescribed by the Model Penal Code.

The principle of parsimony in the use of imprisonment is no longer in doubt, unless doubt is cast upon it by the second fundamental question we face—why not imprison all criminals convicted of serious crime until risk of their recidivism has passed? That question may be deferred, at least temporarily.

2. Dangerousness

In relation to the second principle, that "dangerousness" as a prediction of future criminality is an unjust basis for imposing a sentence of imprisonment, we move from the broadly accepted to the highly contentious. "Dangerousness" must be rejected for this purpose, since it presupposes a capacity to predict future criminal behavior quite beyond our present technical ability. Further, it is clear that in a world of even remote resemblance to our present social organization such predictive capacities will continue to elude us.

There is a seductive appeal to drawing a distinction between the dangerous and the nondangerous and confining imprisonment to the former. It would be such a neat trick if we could perform it: prophylactic punishment—the preemptive judicial strike, scientifically justified—saving potential victims of future crimes and at the same time minimizing the use of imprisonment and reducing the time to be served by most prisoners. But it is a trap. Social consequences are often counter-intuitive. The concept of dangerousness is so plastic and vague—its implementation so imprecise—that it would do little to reduce either the present excessive use of imprisonment or social injury from violent crime.

I am aware that dangerousness as a determinative guide to the use of imprisonment has broad support. It has been accepted by two national commissions, by the American Law Institute, by the American Bar Association, by the National Council on Crime and Delinquency in its Model Sentencing Act and its policy statements, by many commentators and in many criminal codes. So great, indeed, is this weight of authority that plenary reasons for rejecting it must be offered, but the essence of the argument is this: every legitimate claim of society to protection from violent recidivism can with justice be met within the other preconditions to imprisonment that I have suggested. The concept of dangerousness for sentencing purposes is an equivocal principle that leads to gross injustice.

The National Council on Crime and Delinquency, in its official policy statement, maintains that "confinement is necessary only for offenders who, if not confined, would be a serious danger to the public" (1973, p. 449). The NCCD policy statement builds on nearly two decades of legislative reform efforts initiated by the American Law Institute's Model Penal Code. That code has also profoundly influenced the states of Delaware, Illinois, Michigan, New York, New Mexico, and Pennsylvania in reshaping their criminal codes. Other states, for example, Arizona and Missouri, are in the process of similar emulation. And if Congress ever recovers from its atrophy no doubt the new federal criminal code will also have sentencing provisions fashioned after the ALI prototype.

Sometimes that same theme is developed in different and even more apparently acceptable language. The American Assembly's report entitled "Prisoners in America" recommended that "High risk offenders may be required to serve fixed periods of time. Low risk offenders should be released to community-based programs as soon as possible" (*Report*, 1973, p. 7). What could be wrong with that? A great deal, it will be submitted.

A decade of efforts at criminal law reform by Herbert Wechsler, Paul Tappan, Francis Allen, and a small group of scholars and practitioners in the mid-1950s and early 1960s has, after yet another decade, come into its own. It proves to be the most important initiative to bring rationality to the criminal law since the codification efforts of Macaulay and Stephen in the last quarter of the nineteenth century. It gains broad legislative acceptance and broad acceptance by national study groups—in 1967 in the Report of the National Crime Commission, in 1973 in the Report of the National Advisory

Commission on Criminal Justice Standards and Goals. In short, the themes behind the ALI refashioning of sentencing have attracted steady scholarly approval and legislative acceptance.

The themes are the following: First, fines and community-based treatments like probation are, where reasonably applicable, to be preferred to imprisonment as penal sanctions. Second, the range of available prison sentences for felonies should be reduced to three or four categories of gravity. Third, within those categories the grounds on which a court may exercise its discretion to impose a sentence of imprisonment should be defined with some degree of precision. A principal aim throughout, if judges can be persuaded or required to give reasons for their sentences, is to build a common law of sentencing. Provisions for appeal against sentence have similar purposes. Finally, the codes that are the progeny of the American Law Institute's Model Penal Code provide for "extended terms" for certain felons. Extended sentences of imprisonment are to be imposed upon persistent, professional, psychologically disturbed and dangerous, or multiple offenders.

To similar effect are other influential legislative models for sentencing dangerous criminals—the Model Sentencing Act of the Advisory Council of Judges of the National Council on Crime and Delinquency and the sentencing provisions of the American Bar Association's Project on Minimum Standards for Criminal Justice.

These models all have in common an effort to reduce the use of imprisonment as a penal sanction by favoring less drastic punishments, by shortening prison sentences to be imposed on those criminals who have to be imprisoned, and by selecting certain defined categories of criminals for protracted incarceration, largely on grounds of their dangerousness.

A recent express acceptance of the distinction between the nondangerous and the dangerous offender for sentencing purposes is to be found in the Report on Corrections of the National Advisory Commission on Criminal Justice Standards and Goals. That commission recommends that "state penal code revisions should include a provision that the maximum sentence for any offender not specifically found to represent a substantial danger to others should not exceed five years for felonies other than murder" (1973, p. 107). Extended terms beyond five years, indeed up to twenty-five years, may be imposed on the persistent felony offender, the professional criminal, and the dangerous offender (pp. 155–57).

Let me be careful about the present position of the argument. I am making the point that for apparently benevolent purposes a belief in our capacity to predict dangerousness is being relied upon. Only the dangerous are to be imprisoned and only the very dangerous are to be protractedly imprisoned. It is a benevolent purpose, but we are far enough down the road of penal reform to know that benevolent purposes do not guarantee beneficent results.

One can well understand the politics of this taxonomy without accepting the concepts on which it is based. An effort to confine imprisonment to the dangerous has obvious political appeal. And provision of extended sentencing terms for the particularly dangerous may allow us to avoid the worst abuses of the habitual criminal laws and the sexual psychopath laws, which have proved grotesquely unjust in application throughout this country. These political justifications for the use of the concept of dangerousness are indeed sometimes expressly recognized. For example, the report of the National Advisory Commission suggested that "clear authority to sentence the dangerous offender to a long term of incapacitation may induce the legislature to agree more readily to a significantly shorter sentence for the nondangerous offender" (*Corrections*, 1973, p. 156). In other words, let us continue to deal unjustly with a few so that we can persuade the legislature to deal more effectively and fairly with the many!

Let me try to define this issue with some precision before grappling with it. Worldwide, sentences of imprisonment are imposed instead of lesser punishments and the terms of imprisonment are increased beyond what would be justified by the crime that precipitates the exercise of sentencing power on various grounds, including:

—the criminal committed crime before,
—he committed this type of crime before,
—he committed many crimes before,

—he has made a profession of crime,
—he committed many other crimes at about the same time as this one,
—he acted with peculiar brutality in this crime, or used a gun, or has determinedly retained the proceeds of his crime, or
—there has been a recent rash of similar crimes.

And there are other similar grounds for determining that imprisonment is appropriate or for increasing the length of the sentence. All merit consideration, but not now. I set them aside in favor of closer analysis of one other ground which seems to be gaining acceptance both in theory and practice in the United States and Europe. It rests upon a preventive notion, namely, that the crime and what we learn of the criminal lead us to the view that he probably will commit a serious crime of personal violence in the future.

In the second chapter, dealing with parole predictions, a distinction was made between categoric, anamnestic, and intuitive predictions of human behavior. Although, it was submitted, anamnestic predictions may properly be relied on to determine probation and parole conditions, predictions of all three types are irrelevant to fixing the date of parole. For present purposes, the distinctions among these three predictive methods may be ignored since the present submission is that all such predictions provide an unjust base for imposing imprisonment in the first instance or for prolonging its term. Despite the weight of authority supporting the principle of dangerousness, it must be rejected because it presupposes a capacity to predict quite beyond our present or foreseeable technical ability. It is necessary to be careful about the type of prediction at issue. We are not inquiring whether the ill-educated, feckless, vocationally deprived youth living in the ghetto is likely to be involved in crime in the future—of course he is. We are not talking about minor crime or crime in general. The focus is on our capacity to predict crimes of some gravity, mostly crimes of violence to the person.

It is important to note that our predictions can fail in two ways and that we have developed an extremely useful technique to conceal the more troublesome failures from ourselves.

First, the two paths to failure. Let us suppose that we have to predict future violence to the person from among one hundred convicted criminals, and let me invent figures that are far superior to any we can now achieve in practice. Assume that of the one hundred, we select thirty as likely future violent criminals. Despite our prediction of danger, all one hundred are either released or left at large. Their subsequent careers are then followed, and with hypothetical precision we know the results. Of the thirty we predicted as dangerous, twenty did commit serious crimes of violence and ten did not. Of the seventy we declared to be relatively safe, five did commit crimes of physical violence and sixty-five did not.

TABLE 1

Prediction		Result	
		No Violent Crime	Violent Crime
Safe	70	65	5
Violent crime	30	10	20
Total	100	75	25

Reading Table 1 one might claim, "We had 80 percent success in our prediction, successfully preselecting twenty out of the twenty-five who later committed serious crimes of violence." Not bad. Of course, we failed to select five of the one hundred who later proved to be dangerous, but that seems a minor failure compared with the twenty serious crimes we could have prevented. Note, however, that we also failed in another way. We selected ten as dangerous—as likely to commit crimes of violence—but they did not. Had we imprisoned the thirty that we predicted as dangerous, in ten cases we would have failed in our prediction by needlessly detaining them. Put more succinctly, we made twenty true positive predictions of violence and ten false positive predictions.

To increase our claimed 80 percent success—to diminish the number of those we predicted as safe but who turned out to be dangerous—we could certainly increase the number of our true positive predictions of dangerousness, but only at the cost of substantially increasing the number of false positive predictions of dangerousness. There, if you will reflect on it, is the moral dilemma we face: how many false positives can be justified for the sake of preventing crimes by the true positives? I shall return to this dilemma.

Rarely do we have such an opportunity to confront the naked jurisprudential issues in neat hypothetical form. Moreover, we possess an extremely convenient mechanism by which to conceal from ourselves our critical incapacity as predictors—the mask of overprediction. If in doubt, put him in or keep him in. Why risk injury or death to innocent potential victims, particularly since the freedom we are talking about is that of a person who has been convicted of crime? I do not mean to sound pejorative; I would no doubt do the same thing myself. If one is unsure about the likely future violent behavior of a person currently under control and for whom that control can legally be prolonged, the benefit of the doubt had better be given to any future possible victim rather than to the criminal or to the prisoner. What is wonderfully convenient about this overprediction of risk is that the predictor does not know who in particular, as a person, as eyes to be met, he is needlessly holding. Further, he is most unlikely to precipitate any political or administrative trouble as a result of ordering imprisonment or prolonging its duration. By contrast, one is quite likely to be in water too warm for comfort when those people whom one has released, but who could legally have been detained, *do* involve themselves in crimes of violence, particularly if those crimes are sensationally reported. Hence, the path of administrative and political safety is the path of the overpredicted risk.

Another important consequence of the mask of overprediction is that we lack sufficient empirical studies of our predictive capacity. All of us, of course, are masters at retrospective prediction, characterized by the tired phrase "I told you so." We possess 20-20 powers of hindsight; we are less sure of our capacity as prospective predictors. While those we have predicted as dangerous languish in institutions, we are not in a position critically to test our predictions. There have, however, been two recent opportunities critically and scientifically to test the matter. One has occurred by the force of a judicial decision, the other by the diligence of an imaginative and protracted research effort.

The decision of the United States Supreme Court in *Baxstrom v. Herold* (383 U.S. 107) in 1966 created a natural experiment in the overprediction of dangerousness. It is extraordinary that the case could have reached the Supreme Court, so indefensible was the position argued for by the appellant, the State of New York. Psychologically disturbed prisoners were being classified as suitable for detention in the institutions for the criminally insane at Dannemora and Mattewan. Some were held in these institutions beyond the term of their sentence if, after psychiatric examination, they were deemed mentally ill and dangerous to themselves or to others. The Court affirmed the rather obvious proposition that such prisoners could not be held beyond the period of their original criminal sentence without receiving the usual due process protections of the ordinary civil commitment processes, for example, jury trial. When the prisoner's criminal sentence expires, he must be given the same protections as ordinary persons, not just the lesser protections the state extends to mentally ill prisoners. The immediate administrative effect of this banal decision was to compel the release or the transfer to civil mental hospitals pursuant to ordinary civil commitment processes of each of the 967 "Baxstrom patients."

It is important to remember that all of the Baxstrom patients were convicted criminals being held as likely to be dangerous if released. What were the results when these predicted dangerous criminals were released by virtue of the Supreme Court's decision? Several follow-up studies of the later careers of the Baxstrom patients have been pursued. The broad conclusion is that there had been gross overprediction of dangerousness. Perhaps the most intensive study was that done by Dr. Henry Steadman and his associates, which was summarized in their report on "The Baxstrom Patients: Backgrounds and Outcomes" (Steadman and Keveles, 1972). This incorporated a four-year intensive follow-up of the later careers of these 967 transferred or discharged patients. The report concludes, "Two striking facts about the Baxstrom patients are the high proportion [subsequently] released of those transferred to the civil hospitals and the low proportion subsequently readmitted. . . . [D]uring their first year of civil hospitalization the Baxstrom patients were not as troublesome as had been expected. Our findings suggest that they were equally not dangerous after they were released. Between 1966 and 1970, barely 21 of the 967 Baxstrom patients returned to Mattewan or Dannemora. All the findings seriously question the legal and psychiatric structures that retained these 967 people an average of 13 years in institutions for the criminally insane."

The Baxstrom patients certainly proved to be less violent than had been predicted. Only 2 percent were returned to the institutions for the criminally insane between 1966 and 1970, and only 19.6 percent of the males and 25.5 percent of the females were reported to have shown any assaultive behavior in civil hospitals. Their release rate from civil hospitals was higher than that of comparable civilly committed state hospital patients. With respect to their community adjustment, a large number—56 percent of the males and 43 percent of the females—had no subsequent readmission to mental hospitals during the four years of follow-up. Their subsequent criminal activity was low. Thirteen of the 84 released patients for whom there was adequate follow-up information had a total of eighteen criminal contacts with the police. This is a remarkably low rate considering the fact that all of these were held as dangerous criminals, likely to be violent.

In effect, the Supreme Court in *Baxstrom v. Herold* compelled the testing of our predictions of violence, and the test revealed massive overprediction. To regard practice in New York and the institutions of Dannemora and Mattewan as lying outside the mainstream of institutions for the criminally insane would be erroneous. The story of the Baxstrom patients could be told for many of the people we currently hold in prisons and mental hospitals in many parts of the world because we deem them likely to be involved in future violence (Steadman and Cocozza).

So much for the impact of a judicial decision testing predictions of dangerousness; let us now turn to a research project with a similar result. In October 1972, Drs. Harry Kozol, Richard Boucher, and Ralph Garofaio reported (Kozol, 1972) on a ten-year study to test their capacity to define and predict dangerousness. They selected a high risk group of offenders in prison in Massachusetts and then with unusually extensive clinical and social case work resources—independent examinations

in every case by at least two psychiatrists and a social worker—
they endeavored to predict the likely future dangerousness of
each offender prior to his consideration for release. They identified for the releasing authority those offenders who in their
view were dangerous and those who were not. Their thesis was
that "the validity of our diagnostic criteria and the effectiveness
of treatment may be judged by comparing the behavior of patients released on our recommendation with the behavior of
those who were released against our advice" (p. 389). Table 2

TABLE 2

Prediction		Result	
		No Violent Crime	Violent Crime
Safe	386	355	31 (1M)
Violent crime	49	32	17 (2M)
Total	435	387	48

is an effort to summarize the results of the Kozol study (the 1M
and 2M in parentheses in the violent crime result column refer
to one murder and two murders respectively). The Kozol team
was attempting to predict serious assaultive behavior. It will
be seen that they were remarkably effective predictors, functioning at the forefront of our present clinical predictive capacity. The frequency of assaultive behavior was more than
four times greater among those released *against* their advice
than among those released *on* their advice. But consider the
cost that must be paid. Of the forty-nine who were released
against the advice of the Kozol team, thirty-two did not subsequently commit any serious assaultive crimes during five
years of freedom. What it comes to is this: saving each "true
positive," benefiting the community and indeed the offender by
his non-release and therefore non-commission of a serious assaultive crime, requires the detention of two others who were
equally predicted to be involved in serious assaultive behavior
but who, in fact, would not be so involved were they released.
Detention of two false positives is the cost of controlling one
true positive. Kozol and his associates are, of course, fully
aware of this trade-off, and their report is a model of the careful

collection of data that policy makers must have if they are responsibly to face the difficult jurisprudential and ethical problems that underlie the proper use of imprisonment.

Two methodological niceties should be mentioned before the Kozol study is put aside. First, in the Kozol study no effort was made to distribute unreported and undetected serious assaultive crimes between the four outcome groups. Second, there is a further small group, not identified in the study, concealed to an uncertain degree by the mask of overprediction—those predicted by the Kozol team as dangerous and not released by the authorities for follow-up in the community. But since the follow-up covered a five-year period and since all released prisoners had criminal records well known to the police, it is most unlikely that any further statistical data will throw doubt on the broad conclusion from the Kozol study. Even when a high risk group of convicted criminals is selected, and those carefully predicted as dangerous are detained, for every three so incarcerated there is only one who would in fact commit serious assaultive crime if all three were released.

It is important also to appreciate the political danger in the current widespread acceptance of dangerousness as a justification for imposing imprisonment or as a basis for prolonging the duration of a prison term. So imprecise is the concept of dangerousness that the punitively minded will have no difficulty in classifying within it virtually all who currently find their miserable ways to prison and, in addition, many offenders who are currently sentenced to probation or other community-based treatments. If one looks at the grist of the mill of city jails and state felony prisons it is hard not to drop these gnarled grains through the expansive hole of "dangerousness."

That is why the official policy statement of the National Council on Crime and Delinquency that offenders identified in their Model Sentencing Act as dangerous "must be held in secure institutions until it is safe to release them" (NCCD, 1973, p. 456) is so misguided. "Dangerousness" is itself a dangerously expansive rubric.

Yet, it must be admitted, our inability to predict dangerousness with any degree of accuracy and the politically expansive quality of that concept do not compel the abandonment of dangerousness as a determinant of the decision to imprison or of the duration of a prison term. There are those, no doubt, who would accept the cost and willingly incapacitate three convicted offenders from committing crime in the community even if they agreed that only one would indeed do so if released. After all, we cannot know which one, and all three are convicted criminals. Public safety justifies their sacrifice.

Hence, any firm conclusion drawn from these observations on our modest capacity to predict violent behavior must await resolution of the second question addressed in this chapter— why risk future criminality by releasing convicted criminals? My own conclusion may properly be foreshadowed: as a matter of *justice* we should never take power over the convicted criminal on the basis of unreliable predictions of his dangerousness.

3. Desert

The third general principle guiding the decision to imprison dictates a maximum of punishment limited by the concept of desert: no sanction greater than that "deserved" by the last crime or series of crimes for which the offender is being sentenced should be imposed.

This principle, which accepts retributive purposes as a limitation on punishment, is addressed in the literature on the philosophy of punishment (Ewing, 1929; Hart, 1963; Moberly, 1968; Feinberg, 1970). It affirms that, as a matter of justice, the maximum of punishment should never exceed the punishment "deserved," either to cure the criminal or to protect the citizenry. This principle strikes directly at the larger question I have deferred, namely, why not hold all convicted criminals until risk of their recidivism is past? But in the interim brief comment on it is appropriate.

Two distinctions are necessary. First, between desert as related to salvation or ethics, admission to the company of heaven or of men of virtue, and desert as related to social organization as it is, admission or readmission to the company of citizens. Then, discussing desert only in the second sense, as an aid to social organization, a second distinction may be drawn between rejection and expiation.

In the principles here offered and in their later application as preconditions to imprisonment, I am referring to desert in its mundane, social context. George Bernard Shaw put the point neatly: "Vengeance is mine, saith The Lord; which means it is not the Lord Chief Justice's." Insofar as we seek a morally sensitive scale in which to weigh subjective guilt, to classify the individual criminal on the long continuum from unblemished virtue to unmitigated evil, the task is best left either to the Recording Angel or to the delicacies of moral disputation. If all are to get their deserts, in this sense, who will escape whipping? The criminal law is unfitted for such issues. It faces an adequacy of difficulties without addressing such ethical nuances. It is necessarily generalized rather than related to the moral quality of the specific act. The criminal law applies a concept of desert which sometimes assesses the minimum of punishment the convicted offender must suffer if he is to be reaccepted as a member of society but always defines the maximum of punishment that may be inflicted on him.

Here the second distinction becomes operative—between rejection and expiation. Capital punishment, banishment, and life imprisonment, in the strict sense, do not reintegrate the offender into society. It matters less if their severity exceeds what is deserved. They are imposed on the criminal as a means of using him to preserve the social structure—without him! In the language of the convicted felons transported to Australia in the eighteenth century: "We left our country for our country's good."

Imprisonment is not now seen as a permanent social rejection; it is at the most a temporary banishment; the prison gates open for all but a very few. Imprisonment is thus, in terms of this distinction, expiative and not rejective. I do not, of course, suggest that the community rejoices to receive the discharged prisoner as a wandering lamb returned to the fold. The path to his social acceptance is steep and treacherous. But at least imprisonment is intended to have an expiative effect.

The concept of desert in this chapter is thus limited to its use as defining the maximum of punishment that the community exacts from the criminal to express the severity of the injury his crime inflicted on the community as a condition of readmitting him to society. Questions of guilt will thus be weighed on the imprecise scales of the criminal law which can allow for only a few subjective qualifications to the objective gravity of the crime.

The link between established crime and deserved suffering, in that sense, is a central precept of everyone's sense of justice or, to be more precise, of everyone's sense of injustice (Cahn, 1949). To use the innocent as a vehicle for general deterrence would be seen by all as unjust, though it need not be ineffective if the innocence of the punished is concealed from the group threatened. We use only the "guilty" to that deterring end; they have deserved this role and to play it facilitates their readmission to the group. Equally, punishment in excess of what is felt by the community to be the maximum suffering justly related to the harm the criminal has inflicted is, to the extent of that excess, a punishment of the "innocent," inhibiting his readmission to society, though, again, it may be effective for a variety of purposes.

To say that a punishment is deserved, in this sense, is not to say that it ought to be imposed. The concept of desert here advanced is one of a retributive maximum; a license to punish the criminal up to that point but by no means an obligation to do so. For example, the principle of parsimony should also infuse all decisions as to the proper punishment to impose. Mercy, clemency, the avoidance of severing the convicted criminal's social ties by imposing a term of imprisonment, are all values of importance to be served up to the proper limits of the larger social utility. The criminal law has general preventive purposes in relation to crime, cohesive functions in relation to society, educative and deterrent functions in relation to potential criminals, all of which bear upon the determination of the proper punishment. The punishment equation relates these social purposes to the sentence on the convicted criminal up to the deserved punishment. And that is where the American Friends Service Committee went wrong in *Struggle for Justice* with their advocacy of legislatively fixed sentences immune from judicial or other discretions; deserved justice and a discriminating clemency are not irreconcilable.

The concept of desert is a necessary but not sufficient condition of the punishment of crime. Desert is, of course, not precisely quantifiable. There is uncertainty as to the judge's role in its assessment, argument as to the extent to which he ought to reflect legislative and popular views of the gravity of the crime if they differ from his own. And further, views of the proper maximums of retributive punishments differ dramatically between countries, between cultures and subcultural groups, and in all countries over time. Nevertheless, the concept of desert remains an essential link between crime and punishment. Punishment in excess of what is seen by that society at that time as a deserved punishment is tyranny.

A brief excursus on one relationship between predictions of dangerousness and the principles of desert and deterrence is a necessary prelude to a more precise statement of the preconditions to imprisonment.

Predictions of dangerousness are, it has been submitted, to be rejected as a basis for imposing or prolonging a term of imprisonment; yet principles of desert and of deterrence are relevant to that end. What if both the latter incorporate ideas of predicted dangerousness? What then remains of the rejection of predictions of dangerousness as a basis for imprisoning?

These questions are, at first blush, troublesome, but they turn out to be easily answered. A few distinctions are necessary.

Those predictions of dangerousness that should be rejected are individual categoric, anamnestic, or intuitive predictions that this criminal will commit a crime (or a crime of physical violence) if we leave him at large or release him. They are particularized. On the other hand, desert as we have seen is generalized and is not related either to predictions of this man's future behavior or to too close an attention to the pressures that led to his past behavior. Fear may well condition the retributive upper price a community places on a given crime. That fear may reflect the distribution and frequency of that crime in that community. It may respond to a few sensational events. It may respond to a wave of widely reported crimes. It looks backward to what has been done by others or to the brutal or mitigating details of what this criminal has done. It is quantifiable—so far as it is quantifiable—independently of the risk of similar future criminal behavior by this criminal.

Likewise, in later advocating a general deterrent justification for the imposition of a prison sentence, I intend to exclude the fear of repetition of crime by this criminal. The concept is that of general deterrence, not special deterrence: the deterrence of all who might be inclined to do what he has done. It involves no predictions as to his future behavior; it does not seek to imprison him so that he more than others will not do it again.

Preconditions to Imprisonment

To take the matter beyond generalities and to offer a more precise answer to the question of when a sentence of imprisonment may justly be imposed, let me contrast the provisions of the American Law Institute's Model Penal Code, on which all subsequent federal and state proposed and accepted criminal codes have heavily relied, with the subsantially different preconditions to imprisonment I have offered.

The late Paul Tappan was the architect of the ALI Model Penal Code provisions on sentencing and corrections. His contribution to rationality and decency in the criminal justice system is too rarely recognized; so I am reluctant to single out from so much of lasting value in his work on that Code some sections I find analytically unsound and of mischievous consequence. Still, Paul Tappan well understood the Code as a series of political compromises. Opinions have changed; knowledge has advanced, although slowly; and the need to bring principle and clarity of purpose to sentencing has become overwhelmingly clear.

Section 7.01 of the Proposed Official Draft of the ALI Model Penal Code directs the court not to sentence the convicted criminal to imprisonment unless:

(a) there is undue risk that during the period of a
    suspended sentence or probation the defendant will
    commit another crime; or
(b) the defendant is in need of correctional treatment
    that can be provided most effectively by his
    commitment to an institution; or
(c) a lesser sentence will depreciate the seriousness
    of the defendant's crime.

Later state and federal reforms of sentencing practice have built upon and in varying degree adopted these three criteria for resolving the question of whether or not to imprison.

As we have seen, criterion (a) is entirely unacceptable as a matter of principle. We lack the capacity to predict dangerousness that this criterion assumes and, even if we could predict with substantially greater precision, to take power based on such a prediction is, as discussed below, an abuse of human rights.

The second criterion—the need for correctional treatment— unambiguously accepts the worst assumptions underlying the rehabilitative ideal. It too must be rejected as an abuse of power. It would be repetitive in the extreme to set out yet again the many objections to this reliance on coercively curing criminals in prison.

The third criterion—that any punishment other than imprisonment would depreciate the seriousness of the defendant's crime (sometimes expressed, "that imprisonment is necessary to deprecate the crime")—has received universal acceptance, and, currently at least, provides an unavoidable justification for imprisonment. It reflects the obverse of the argument of the maximum deserved punishment as a ceiling to punishment. Retribution, socialized under the criminal law from its roots in individual vengeance, not only limits the worst suffering we can inflict on the criminal, but also sometimes dictates the minimum sanction a community will tolerate. For example, the typical wife slayer convicted of murder is most unlikely to be involved in future criminality, would be a safe bet under Model Penal Code criterion (a) were it acceptable and probably needs none of the retraining contemplated by criterion (b), since the crime itself may well have solved his outstanding emotional problems. Nonetheless, he cannot, as a routine matter, be put on probation or given a suspended sentence even were a showing made that the incidence of wife slaying would not increase consequent upon a reduction of the frequency of imprisonment of wife slayers. The criminal law has general behavioral standard-setting functions; it acts as a moral teacher; and, consequently, requires a retributive floor to punishment as well as a retributive ceiling.

If only one of the Model Penal Code criteria is acceptable, what is to be substituted? The three criteria I have offered could form the foundation for a jurisprudence of the decision to imprison if legislatures and courts cared to move to create a statutory and common law of imprisoning, which is now lacking.

The first criterion I have suggested is taken directly from the Model Penal Code and requires only brief amplification. Imprisonment is the least restrictive punishment appropriate to this case because any lesser punishment would depreciate the seriousness of the crime(s) committed. An example of a typical murderer has been suggested; many others come to mind based on the brutality of the crime or the particular circumstances or notoriety of the criminal. Many white-collar crimes or crimes by those in situations of public responsibility or high public office belong to this category. It is, in brief, the lowest level of clemency tolerable under current punitive mores (Spiro Agnew strained at its boundary).

The second criterion I have suggested—that of the necessities of general deterrence and the appropriateness of this offender for deterrent purposes—finds no place in current codes but remains, in my view, inescapable (Zimring, 1971; Zimring and Hawkins, 1973; Andenaes, 1974). It is, for example, the principle on which rests the entire structure of income tax sanctions. Not every tax felon need be imprisoned, only a number sufficient to keep the law's promises and to encourage the rest of us to honesty in our tax returns. The present arrangements for imprisoning federal tax offenders are an object lesson in the parsimonious application of general deterrent sanctions: approximately 80 million tax returns were filed in 1972; only 43 percent of the 825 individuals convicted for tax fraud were jailed (Commissioner of Internal Revenue, *Annual Report* 1972, pp. 18–19).

General deterrent purposes are also justified in many other areas of the criminal law, although they will frequently not call for imprisonment in areas serving merely regulatory purposes. The limitation of the maximum deserved punishment for the particular offender precludes imprisonment in this context unless, of course, the violation follows repeated breaches of the law, in which event the third suggested justification will apply.

The third criterion for imposing imprisonment concerns cases in which lesser sanctions have frequently or recently been imposed on a given offender for earlier bouts of crime. This *faute de mieux* criterion is also subject to a retributive maximum; no repetition of the entirely inconsequential should lead to imprisonment. However, there must be a role for the residual penal sanction, imprisonment, if the lesser sanctions have been appropriately applied and contumaciously ignored and the offender comes yet again for punishment. Here too the criminal law must keep its retributive promises, although it need not be precipitate in moving to its heavy weaponry.

These principles—the least restrictive sanction; imprisonment only when any alternative punishment would depreciate the seriousness of the crime, or when imprisonment is necessary for general deterrence, or when all else practicable has been applied; the whole limited by a concept of the maximum deserved punishment—offer a basis on which a rational and parsimonious use may be made of imprisonment.

One last comment is pertinent. No principled jurisprudence of sentencing will emerge before legislatures bring order to the penal provisions in their statute books or before judges routinely give reasons for the sentences they impose. Only in this manner can the broad and detailed sweep of a common law of sentencing evolve.

II. WHY SHOULD WE RISK FUTURE CRIMINALITY BY CONVICTED CRIMINALS?

Why should we not try coercively to "cure" criminals, either in the therapeutic sense of changing their behavior or in the sense of insulating ourselves from their future depredations? Is opposition to such cures a question of our inability to achieve them or an acknowledgment that it would cost too much? Or are there other reasons? Suppose we could, by an injection invented tomorrow, transform the criminal lion to the conforming lamb? And for "cures" in the second sense—protecting the unconvicted from the convicted—we have the machinery at hand. Capital punishment is an unfailingly successful cure; castration, either surgically or chemically achieved, substantially diminishes rape-specific recidivism. Virtually all criminals can have their subsequent violent crime dramatically reduced by detaining them in prison until their fiftieth birthdays. Why should we not detain all offenders predicted to be dangerous beyond whatever is the just maximum period of punishment by imprisonment for what they have done? After all, such imprisonment will, as was adequately demonstrated by the Kozol study, protect from serious personal injury the likely victims of at least one of each three so detained. Surely, many will argue, thus to prevent serious crime justifies protracted incarceration of those who are, after all, convicted felons.

The question pushes us to fundamentals. The answer depends, I suggest, on the frame of reference of the question. Protracted incarceration of those predicted to be dangerous would diminish crime and need not be rejected because of any sentimental concern for their welfare. If the discussion of values be confined to the criminal law, surely imprisonment beyond the otherwise just punishment may be based on current predictions of dangerousness. We can in this way prevent some serious crimes of violence—and those who pay the cost of the gradual capital punishment that is protracted imprisonment are not particularly valuable citizens anyhow. And the community seems prepared to meet the relatively small costs of providing the prison cages; it seems, if anything, delighted to do so.

But a different frame of reference leads to a different answer. Such punishments should be opposed because of fundamental views of human freedoms, rights, and dignities. We do not suspect, we know, that respect for the human condition requires drawing precise, justiciable restraints on powers assumed over other persons. Slavery, in certain settings, provides a clearly desirable social and economic way of life—for other than the slaves. We reject it for a larger view of man and society in which we affirm dogmatic principles governing human rights and, to the best of our political abilities, protect them. Fairness and justice, not a generalized cost-benefit utilitarian weighing, dictate the choice.

In *A Theory of Justice*, John Rawls develops important jurisprudential themes relevant to the question we are now addressing. His "Main Idea" is particularly germane.

Readers unacquainted with Rawls's theory may be assisted by a summary of this "Main Idea." Such summarization is a task not to be attempted without an intellectual safety net. So, let me offer the words of H. L. A. Hart to this end: "Principles of justice do not rest on mere intuition yet are not to be derived from utilitarian principles or any other teleological theory holding that there is some form of good to be sought and maximized. Instead, the principles of justice are to be conceived as those that free and rational persons concerned to further their own interests would agree should govern their forms of social life and institutions if they had to choose such principles from behind 'a veil of ignorance'—that is, in ignorance of their own abilities, of their psychological propensities and conception of the good, and of their status and position in society and the level of development of the society of which they are to be members. The position of these choosing parties is called 'the original position' " (Hart, 1973, p. 535).

In his "original position" Rawls does not consider the prisoner as within the social group properly to be described as "the least advantaged" whose interests, since each contracting party might be a member of that group, will dictate the maximum adversities to be inflicted on anyone. He therefore never reaches the problem we now face; indeed, he expressly avoids the prisoner's relationship to "justice as fairness." Specifically, Rawls considers "strict compliance (or ideal) as opposed to partial compliance theory. . . . The latter studies the principles that govern how we are to deal with injustice. . . . Obviously the problems of partial compliance theory are the pressing and urgent matters. These are the things that we are faced with in everyday life. The reason for beginning with ideal theory is that it provides, I believe, the only basis for the systematic grasp of these more pressing problems" (Rawls, 1971, pp. 8–9). I am, therefore, encouraged—with confidence in the value of the inquiry if not in the precision of my argument—to suggest that the same principles that move beyond utilitarian analysis in the assessment of justice in strict compliance legal theory are also applicable to criminal punishments and limit imprisonment in its application and duration to what is deserved by the crime rather than what is feared from the prisoner.

Should prisoners be included at the "original position" among the group of "free and rational persons concerned to further their own interests . . . in an initial position of equality" (Rawls, 1971, p. 11)? Such persons are, of course, behind "the veil of ignorance" that characterizes contracting at the original position and are ignorant of their own abilities and social positions and standing. Suppose we make them ignorant too of whether they will be prisoners and ask them to settle fair and just criteria for imprisonment. Of course, it could be argued that by one's behavior one can choose not to be a prisoner and therefore, at the original position, no one would identify himself as possibly a prisoner and would not egocentrically consider minimum standards for prison and imprisoning.

This seems a much too narrow view. I could swiftly persuade a mass of "original position contractors" (quite apart from any imprecise sentiments about "there, but for the Grace of God, go I") that they might well be born into a highly criminogenic social group—a disrupted family setting in an underclass whose life experiences are typified by fortuitous involvements in crime—bearing substantial risks of imprisonment for serious crime. Since all human behavior is the product of interaction between endogenous processes and exogenous pressures and circumstances, the blanket exclusion of prisoners from Rawls's "worst-off members of society" on grounds of a purported dominance of the individual's rationality and self-determination is unfounded. In considering prisons and prisoners from behind the veil of ignorance, therefore, we should include ourselves as potentially within the prison population; we would, in that context, subscribe to concepts of fairness and justice that preclude the sacrifice of the individual prisoner to a supposed larger social good.

Whatever my lack of clarity in relating Rawls's fundamental principles of justice to the sentencing of convicted criminals, and to the proper limits of imprisonment and prison punishments, this much seems clear: not only lack of knowledge forces us to hesitate to impose dramatic or Draconian "cures" on criminals; basic views of the minimum freedoms and dignities rightfully accorded human beings stay our punitive hands.

Utilitarian values, of course, also limit punitive excess. Were the punishment for the most trivial crime as severe as that for the most serious, any efficacy in differential deterrence or in the reprobative and educative force of the criminal law would dissipate. Nonetheless, the chief limitation remains our view of justice as fairness, according defined minimum freedoms and dignities to man *qua* man. The perception that abuse of governmental power is a central problem of the human condition and that treatment of the criminal is closely bound to that problem serves as the fundamental inhibitor of punitive excess.

A proper cynicism about the likely abuse of power compels a limitation on maximum control over the criminal to that justified, wholly apart from considerations of curing him of his crime or protecting the rest of us permanently from future risk. If criminals are to be coercively cured today, we all know that the rest of us may tomorrow be regarded as in need of remedial training, both to achieve our maximum social potential and to minimize the collateral injuries to others we all scatter along our devious paths. If criminals, if the mentally ill or the retarded are subjected to coercive control beyond that justified by the past injuries they have inflicted, then why not you, and certainly me? We find ourselves in the business of remaking man, and that is beyond our competence; it is an empyrean rather than an earthly task.

4

A Prison for
Repetitively Violent Criminals

Some of the principles offered in this book for a new model of imprisonment would require legislative acceptance for their implementation; others fall within the competence of the judiciary or the parole board or the prison administration. Self-delusion does not lead me to the view that there will be a precipitate rush to overall application of my model. At best it may merit scholarly criticism and cautious testing. Therefore, it seems sensible in this last chapter to suggest a way in which some of these principles could now be applied, without legislative change or judicial acceptance, by any correctional administration and parole board that thought them worth testing.

Too many prison reform programs have the research defect of selecting the least troublesome and difficult group of prisoners in order to demonstrate that they can be treated in less restrictive and less punitive ways, to their advantage and to the advantage of the community generally. Projects of this nature always succeed. They succeed in that they are designed in a fashion that guarantees their success. There is no trick at all in demonstrating that too many criminals are sent to prison and that one can select out from the prison population a group who will have lesser recidivism rates if they are treated on probation, or certainly that their recidivism rates will be no higher and that it is cheaper to treat them in the community than behind the walls. But if some measure of success can be achieved by reforms applied to the toughest group of inmates, their feasibility should be established as to the entire prison system.

Repetitively violent criminals cannot be regarded as those most likely to succeed—except perhaps at returning to prison. But this rejection of a test which would achieve a spurious success is not a sufficient justification for selecting *this* group; further reasons for their selection will be offered.

The sequence of presentation of this outline plan for a prison for repetitively violent criminals is:

1. Why Plan Such an Institution?
2. Selection of the Group
3. Intake and Release Procedures
4. Staff Selection and Training
5. Institutional Program and Living Units
6. Evaluation

A preliminary caveat must be entered. This chapter is not intended to be a detailed operational plan of a proposed prison, from physical structure to daily program. Rather, it is a sketch of how already recommended principles of imprisonment might promptly be applied to, and tested on, a defined group of prisoners. It is the conceptual foundation on which a detailed architectural and operational plan could be designed.

1. *Why Plan Such an Institution?*

It may seem an obvious question. After all, the prototypical criminal in the public's mind, the criminal generating the most pervasive fear, is the violent criminal. And within the universe of criminals convicted of violent crimes there are some who account for a disproportionately large number of violent offenses. This group of repetitively violent offenders is a source of anxiety within the prison walls as well as in society-at-large. Prison security measures are generally geared to those who present the most serious threat of violence and thus the daily routine of other inmates and of prison staff is restricted by measures designed to control the relatively few aggressive and dangerous prisoners. Even among the prison affiliates of ghetto street gangs, where controlled violent behavior is often valued and encouraged, certain gang members are recognized by others as being irrationally and repetitively violent, and this is a matter of concern to the gang leaders. Finally, repetitively violent behavior is often a cause of great anguish to the offender himself. But simply because such prisoners exist does not require that they be gathered together in a special facility; it may be wiser to disperse them among the prison population than to concentrate them in one institution; at least the matter cannot be taken for granted.

As we have seen, the existence of a group of dangerous and violent criminals is assumed in the current wave of criminal code reform. The statutory models and drafts of the last few years have proposed, and many states have adopted, sentencing structures providing for shorter sentences for most individuals convicted of crimes. However, while decreasing the periods of imprisonment for the run-of-the-mill criminal, these codes authorize extended sentences, typically up to twice the maximum sentence for the crime committed, for a group of offenders which is differently described in the various codes but which generally includes the persistent, the professional, and the dangerous offender.

In the discussion and literature advocating the adoption of these statutes the focus has been on the trade-off advantages of the liberalizing effect on the majority of the prison population of this reduction of sentences for the many and lengthening of sentences for the few. Somewhat unfairly, those singled out for longer terms of imprisonment have been largely ignored in the commentary to the codes, except in terms of stressing the harm they inflict on society. It is a purpose of this chapter to try to fill the gap by suggesting what should be done with at least one category of those sentenced to extended terms. If we select certain prisoners to bear the burden of heavier sentences so that the remainder of the prison population may be released earlier and treated in less punitive circumstances, surely we have a moral obligation at least to allow those serving extended terms an opportunity to make some constructive use of the time we have demanded of them. And unless we intend to lock them away forever, our reasons for attempting to rehabilitate these prisoners are not only moral but eminently practical.

Several benefits to the corrections system as a whole may be anticipated from establishing a special prison for the repetitively violent. First, removal of a few threatening inmates from the general prison population will mean that security measures in other institutions may be reduced. Of course, this "ease up" effect on existing prisons may be felt whether or not the proposed institution is itself successful, since it may result from the mere transfer of these offenders rather than from any beneficial treatment or effect on the offenders themselves, but it is an advantage nonetheless.

There is another more important and subtle contribution that the institution may make to corrections in general. The point was summarized by a critic of the Herstedvester institution in Denmark and of Dr. Georg Stürup, who had, in effect, created that institution. The critic said: "At least Stürup demonstrated that the most dangerous prisoners could be treated decently, humanely. And if them, then all other prisoners also." The point is that if a humane and reformative program can be accorded to this category of offenders, then it should have as a direct and inescapable consequence the application of better programs throughout the prison system to less threatening groups. This "deep-end" approach is justified, therefore, both as an experimental technique and for its long-range general influence on penal practice.

There are, of course, serious political problems in planning a prison for the repetitively violent, especially if it leads to the construction of a new prison rather than the remodeling of an existing institution. The plan is being offered at a time when, as we have seen, powerful voices are advocating a moratorium on the construction of any new penal institutions and when there is also substantial advocacy of the abolition of imprisonment itself. Still, few suggest viable alternative punishments for this group of offenders. And standing in polar opposition to these reformers, there are some prison administrators who stress the need to create small maximum security facilities for the most troublesome offenders—"maxi-maxi" institutions. Their plans read like the design of the inner circles of hell. This move toward the maxi-maxi institution is, it is submitted, as counter-productive as is the simplistic belief in the withering away of the prison itself.

This plan for a new institution for repetitively violent offenders is likely to be attacked both from the left and the right; from the left as impeding the abatement of imprisonment, from the right as providing impossibly permissive alternatives ·to the needed maxi-maxis. There is a long history of the perversion of decent plans in correctional reform; there is a genuine risk that the proposals we are developing may raise false hopes and may be misapplied; that additional cages will be provided and quickly filled. But, as was argued earlier, it would be stultifying to stay all reformative effort through fear of its potential abuse.

Another danger in establishing an institution for serious offenders is that wardens of other prisons will, if past behavior is any guide, attempt to use the new institution as a dumping ground for the troublemakers in their own prisons, simply to make their own inmate population more manageable. The selection system later proposed will greatly reduce this possibility for abuse since inmates will be randomly selected from an objectively defined pool and will further be given the opportunity to reject longer-term placement in the special institution.

These gloomy political anxieties should not impede rational planning. All commentators seem to agree that for many generations to come there will be a residue of convicted criminals whom society will need to incarcerate, no matter how generous the political community becomes with the provision of correctional services. Rational and humane planning for this group should set free resources of intelligence, decency, and efficiency for the correctional treatment of all convicted criminals. If we can rehabilitate the rehabilitative ideal with these prisoners, a humane and effective prison system may not be beyond our grasp.

It may assist critical understanding of the proposed prison for repetitively violent criminals if an effort is now made to outline in a few paragraphs the plan which will later be developed in more detail.

An institution for two hundred prisoners is proposed with maximum security at its perimeter but with a great deal of privacy and freedom of movement within. All inmates will be between the ages of eighteen and thirty-five, will have records of at least two convictions for violent crimes, and will be within three years of their first possible parole date. They will be "volunteers" in the institution in the sense that though they will be randomly selected for admission, they will have the choice within the first four to six weeks in the institution to return to ordinary prisons without suffering any adverse consequences of rejecting the new institution.

A wide diversity of programs will be available in the prison, but the only treatment program in which participation will be obligatory is involvement in a small living and discussion group of eight inmates and two to four staff members. In the first four to six weeks of the prisoner's admission to the institution he will be advised when, on condition only of his avoiding conviction for major disciplinary offenses in the institution, he will be released on parole, when he will be given the opportunity of his first furlough, when his first work release, when his first pre-release placement. The prisoner will, in other words, be fully informed of the duration and conditions of his incarceration in the new facility and will be set free to volunteer in a true sense for its treatment programs. Release and after-care supervision will be intensive. The primary agents facilitating the self-change of the prisoner toward less violent behavior after his release will be the front-of-the-line staff members and the peer pressure and support of his living group. Minority groups will be represented at all levels of staff in approximate proportion to their representation among inmates. A substantial number of all staff positions will be held by women.

The institution will be a success if it reduces the incidence and severity of later violent criminal behavior by those who are randomly selected for its program. An ongoing independent evaluation team should be established to collect and evaluate data on the effect of the institution on recidivism rates of the test and control groups, as well as its effect on its staff, other correctional institutions, and the general community.

It must be recognized that the establishment of such a new correctional facility will require careful collaboration with a variety of interest groups in the community interfacing with the prison authorities, ranging from interested legislators to a variety of citizen groups. The parole board is of particular importance in these discussions; indeed, the willingness of the parole board to assist in giving the prisoners admitted to this institution early decisions on their parole date is essential to the plan. As we have seen, the development of parole contract agreements in Arizona, California, and Wisconsin, by which parole boards of those states have collaborated in somewhat similar arrangements involving early determination of parole dates, gives hope that such cooperation could also be achieved elsewhere.

2. *Selection of the Group*

A group of the more dangerous and violent offenders should be selected for the proposed institution for two reasons: First, this institution will involve a heavy concentration of resources, which is most justifiable, and hence more politically acceptable, if applied to more dangerous offenders. Second, the demonstration of the effectiveness of the proposed institution will be more convincing if it deals with a group of offenders who seriously threaten and disturb the community rather than with a less troublesome group.

Prisoners selected for this institution must be young enough to present a continuing threat of violence in the future; they must be capable of relating to the therapeutic milieu in the proposed institution; and their selection must not frustrate other proper purposes of the prison system from which they are selected.

It might be suggested that the selection of a group of prisoners for this institution based on their predicted future dangerousness offends one of the principles of sentencing earlier advanced, namely, that "prediction of future criminality is an unjust basis for determining that the convicted criminal should be imprisoned." But this is not so. No extra power over the prisoner is taken, his sentence is not prolonged, as a result of this prediction. Further it is not an individual prediction. It is a group prediction, categoric and not anamnestic. It is designed to bring to the institution a group with a high base expectancy failure rate. The selection processes recommended thus involve neither statistical nor ethical errors by building on this type of prediction of dangerousness.

A relatively younger group of prisoners with past records of repeated crimes of violence should be selected. The accuracy of positive predictions of violence from those who have committed several violent acts in the past is significantly greater than the accuracy of similar predictions based on single acts of violence. Likewise, there is abundant evidence that violent behavior tends to fall off as the forties are reached. Selection of an older group for the institution would have a gratifying effect on violent recidivism ("happy the physician who attends the declension of the disease"), but it would again produce only a spurious success for the institution.

Hence we reach a first definition of the group from among whom selection is to be made for placement in the proposed institution: prisoners aged between eighteen and thirty-five who have been twice convicted of serious crimes of personal violence during the last three years they have been at large in the community.

Why use the criterion of conviction? The short answer is that it is the only reliable available basis. Granted the severe distortions due to lack of detection, arbitrariness of arrest, prosecution and conviction, and plea bargaining, what other acceptable evidence of past violent behavior do we have? To be sure, these distortions may lead to a failure to select as many dangerous offenders as we could have selected. But such underprediction is not crucial to the enterprise; we do not need to select the most dangerous or all of the dangerous. The failure to select the most dangerous or all of the dangerous simply makes it that much harder to compare recidivism rates and to find any significant differences between the dangerous group and the general population of offenders, since the recidivism of the latter will be increased by the members of the dangerous group in it. In any case, the effects of such distortions will be randomly distributed between the experimental and control groups and thus will not skew the evaluation of the proposed institution.

It is desirable to exclude from the group from whom the random selection of potential volunteers is to be made those who are psychotic or severely retarded, those who have received extraordinary publicity and the leaders of gangs, militant groups, or organized crime. The reasons for these exclusions are the following: The psychotic and the severely retarded are not likely to benefit substantially from the proposed institution. In addition, there are or should be other mental health facilities for the treatment of such persons and therefore the resources of the new institution should not be diluted to duplicate such facilities.

The notorious, those whose crimes or other aspects of their lives have received extensive publicity, should be excluded from the group from whom the random selection is made since in the small population of the proposed institution their presence and the consequent public attention unnecessarily complicates the life of the institution. Certainly in the early years of this facility a few such notorious cases could have a disruptive effect both within the institution and on its public acceptance.

The leaders of gangs, militant groups, and organized crime should likewise be excluded. They create violence which is less amenable to individualized treatment since it is basically situational. Further, such leaders are motivated more by either ideological or professional considerations which lie outside the treatment purposes of this institution. In addition, the introduction of the leaders of such external organizations has a disruptive effect on the prison.

Selection for the institution should be made only from those prisoners for whom it can be arranged that they will be released on parole between one year and three years of coming to the proposed new prison. The minimum of a year to serve before parole is designed to allow for substantial exposure to institutional programs and to prevent the institution's becoming merely a routine administrative release procedure. The maximum of three years to serve is designed to exclude for the time being those whose parole date is so remote that they may be less motivated to plan realistically for release. In addition, the effect on each prisoner of the relative nearness of release should both lend an air of hope or qualified optimism to the whole institution and temper any preoccupation with survival in or escape from the prison situation. It will also facilitate sharing of experience in planning for release and in a variety of pre-parole, furlough, working out, and community-based placements.

A final dogmatic statement must be made about selection of the group for the institution prior to discussion of some of the problems in selection: All inmates of the institution will be "volunteers" in a sense that will be set out hereunder.

Many other selection criteria might have been chosen that would increase the likelihood of the individual's benefiting from the institution. For example, selection of prisoners with social and family ties still intact, or selection of those who have not lived in institutions for long periods of time, or selection of those whose home is (or was) reasonably near the institution, or, of course, leaving the selection to clinical judgments. I have chosen to elevate none of these to the status of criteria of selection. They are part of what is being studied and it is error to incorporate them into the design; they are better left to distribute themselves randomly between the control and experimental groups. This logic does not preclude the imposition of the selection criterion of between one and three years to serve before parole date. All prisoners will become eligible for selection under this criterion at some stage of their prison careers so that outcome evaluative statistics will not be biased.

It will be noted that it has not been thought necessary to exclude "troublemakers," institutional disciplinary offenders who otherwise meet the selection criteria, from the pool from whom the random selection will be made. There is no need for such a separate exclusion to guard against "dumping" of troublemakers by wardens of other prisons tired of their presence since their institutions do not do the selecting for the new prison under the proposed plan. To the extent that those selected under the community offense-based criteria are also troublemakers, then the institution will have to deal with them. There is no data to suggest that these two groups are composed of the same individuals. In addition, part of the point of the institution is to demonstrate that "troublemakers" can be handled effectively in the milieu which is to be created.

The exclusion of in-prison violence as a selection criterion, even in-prison violence established formally by disciplinary procedures of due process adequacy, is of importance. Using in-prison violence as a criterion would increase the extent to which the institution might be used as a dumping ground for trouble-makers by those responsible for running other prisons. It may well be found that as the institution matures it is capable of encompassing within its selection criteria violence expressed by criminals within the prison as well as at large on the streets. But to start with, the formula I have offered will ensure a random selection of repetitive and serious criminals without distorting it by allowing the institution to be a dumping ground for those whom other prison wardens seek to export.

It is an integral and essential part of this proposal that the institution should never grow to exceed a population of more than two hundred prisoners. A smaller prison would be prefer-able, but some politically acceptable balance between cost and effectiveness must be struck. Too many institutions have been overrun by the burgeoning of populations they were designed to serve.

Assuming then, which will certainly be the case in most states, that there is a substantial oversupply of prisoners fitting the above criteria of suitability for this proposed institution (eighteen to thirty-five; two crimes of violence over three years at large; not psychotic, retarded, or notorious leaders of gangs, militant groups, and organized crime; with one to three years to serve to parole), how is a selection to be made of those to be admitted?

The prime consideration is the need to evaluate the effective-ness of the institution. If the basic assumption or hypothesis of our treatment program is that most offenders will respond positively to the general therapeutic milieu we are trying to create and that specialized treatment for specific identifiable needs is best provided within that milieu, then we have no basis for choosing one individual as against another for the institution. On moral grounds we have no right arbitrarialy to grant to one individual and withhold from another the oppor-tunity for self-change and more humane treatment which we hope the institution will offer. The fairest way to choose our population from the predictively selected and qualifying popula-tion would seem to be by chance.

The obvious advantage of random selection is that we thereby create an experimental group (those chosen for the institution) and a control group (those predicted as dangerous but not chosen for the institution). The control group would presumably be treated in the ordinary way in the prison system which is, in fact, what we want to measure the new institution against in terms of recidivism and a variety of other personal, institutional, and community outcome measures.

It is both practicable and sensible to combine random selection of prisoners from a defined pool with the ideal and reality of their "volunteering" for the proposed institution. These apparently contradictory aims are quite reconcilable. Any concept of treatment or self-change which depends largely on introspection, insight, understanding, self-reliance, and an expanding sense of responsibility, necessarily involves the element of individual motivation. For this reason the individuals selected for the institution ought to be volunteers. Voluntary consent is, of course, meaningless if it is coerced (for example, the prison troublemaker being told to volunteer by guards), if it is bought (for example, by the real or perceived promise of early release or an easier life in prison), or if it is uninformed. Those prisoners who are chosen randomly from within the group that fit the selection criteria set out above ought to be given the opportunity to remove themselves from the new institution at any time after they have had an opportunity to find out for themselves what it is like to serve time there.

The selected prisoners should come to the institution for a period of four to six weeks to find out what the institution is really like—long enough to see beyond the physical surroundings to the hard work and discipline of serious introspection and the prospect of facing one's own problems. During this time the exact nature of the institution would be set out by, in effect, negotiating an individualized contract with each prisoner based on his past, his present situation, and his anamnestic prognosis. "Negotiation" may imply that the inmate has more power than he would over the terms of the document—perhaps one should say that the document would be reviewed and discussed with him. The inmate must be granted the ultimate power to reject the document, although no power to dictate its terms. This document would set out the disciplinary rules within the institution and the reasons for them, the nature and purpose of the treatment programs, the timing and specific requisites for furloughs, work release, the contingencies upon which they would be terminated and the progressive phases of release. The period of settling this contract will be one of intense communication and self-examination and of integration into the small treatment group with which the prisoner will be associated; it ought to give him a clear idea of what the institution will be like for him if he decides to stay.

After the contract is negotiated the prisoner would have the opportunity to sign it or decline to do so. The institution would not have the option to refuse the contract because it would already have had the opportunity to place all of its conditions in the contract to be signed. Those prisoners who do not agree to the contract will simply be returned to the regular prison system. But for them the four- to six-week period would not have been wasted. For them it would have been a period of intense therapy, thought, and discussion. Their views about this institution will, of course, be passed around the prisons to which they return. It is essential that there be no adverse consequences flowing to them from their decision not to stay. This must be stressed. They take back with them to the rest of the prison system their agreed parole and furlough dates. Further, it is important that the Department of Corrections takes care to protect the prisoner who has rejected the proposed institution from any punitive consequences of that rejection during his time in other institutions.

Of course, it must be recognized that the "failures" of the proposed institution, as well as those who reject it and later "fail," may well suffer adverse consequences in terms of increased severity in any future sentences imposed on them for future crimes. But these are marginal and unavoidable consequences of every new treatment effort. They do not unfairly distinguish between those who accept placement in the proposed institution and later commit crime and those who do so after rejecting such placement.

This structure of random selection and volunteering assumes that self-change is unlikely to be facilitated by the milieu of the new institution without the volition of the prisoner. In order to allow for the true consent of those who volunteer, we must necessarily allow the option of not volunteering with no adverse consequences. In the final analysis we must console ourselves with the thought that coerced treatment has been tried and failed often enough in the past.

In considering volunteering as a way to ensure motivation toward self-change we cannot ignore the difficult problem of what it is that the prisoners will think they are volunteering for. We have already alluded to the problem of prisoners volunteering simply to get a more comfortable prison environment. This is an unavoidable problem, unless we choose deliberately to re-create the worst of prison conditions, which would be absurd. Further, the new prison will maintain the right, for cause shown and with proper procedures defined in the contract, to return the prisoner to the general prison population for breach of certain defined conditions of his contract, for example, an act of physical violence within the institution.

A difficult and more subtle and pervasive problem is the prisoners' understanding of how they have been labeled and classified by being selected for the proposed institution. In many European and American institutions the classification of prisoners for admission to these types of prisons is based on psychiatric assessment of psychological disturbance. To put no delicacy on the matter, the prisoners and the staff alike see these institutions as "nut-houses within the prison system." Those running these prisons do their best, of course, and with varying success, to diminish the impact of this negative self-image. The European models are less troubled by this problem since it would appear to the outside observer that the stigmatizing effect of the psychiatric label is much less in western Europe than it is in the United States. But that is certainly one image of the institution—the prison mental hospital—which it is of first importance for these plans to avoid in this country.

There is a Scylla to this Charybdis. The institution must also avoid the "machismo" image. The prisoners must not see themselves, and certainly the staff must not see them, as the *most* dangerous offenders. If the self-image is that of the toughest, the most dangerous, then there is no possibility of creating a supportive, peaceful milieu.

It is my hope that the selection criteria and volunteering procedures outlined above have avoided both these problems. In effect, the image that the prisoners should have of themselves, and that the staff should have of them, would be something like this: "True, all of you have substantial records of convictions for serious crimes of personal violence. We are able to allocate these substantial resources for your treatment in this institution because the community sees you as a particularly troublesome group. However, you are by no means unique. We selected you at random from many hundreds of other prisoners who might as well be here, and you have volunteered to stay here. We are simply trying to find out if a prison run like this one helps those of you who don't want to be convicted of crimes of violence later, to live in the outside community (whatever it is like) without such convictions and to find out whether we can protect the community from violent behavior by people like you when they get out, better than other prisons do. You are not chosen because you are mentally different, or different in terms of your behavior from the run-of-the-mill of serious criminals in this state; you have been chosen largely by chance, randomly from a larger and equally troublesome group."

How does the group of selected nonvolunteers affect the evaluation design? Clearly they constitute a third group: those selected for the experimental group but then nonrandomly assigned back to the control group. They are not a part of the control group. They must be treated as part of the experimental group for purposes of overall evaluation. The same is true of those returned to the general population against their wishes by those running the new prison. As a methodological point: the "treatment" which is being tested in the proposed prison is the total "black box" of everything which is done to and for all who are randomly selected for this prison, including those who reject its treatment and those who are rejected. The control group is all the rest of the qualifying prisoners who are randomly not given the chance to come to or to stay in this new prison.

A final point on the selection of prisoners for this model prison. These plans were discussed at a two-day conference where prison administrators of experience in running similar institutions in Denmark, England, Holland, and the United States met with those responsible for planning such an institution in Illinois and with representatives of the Illinois Department of Corrections. At this conference much attention was given to the question of the inclusion or exclusion from the proposed institution of women offenders who otherwise met the criteria of selection. Given that the staff of the institution will include a large number of women, and given the acceptance of the desirability of women's presence in the institution in its normalizing effect on the life of the institution and its tendency to decrease violence, *prima facie* there would seem to be a case for inclusion of women offenders. There are, however, very few women prisoners who would fit the selection criteria. It was the view of the majority of those at the conference that if only three or four women could be found to be part of the population of this prison of one hundred fifty to two hundred, their inclusion would have no beneficial effects on the life of the institution, would tend to distort the pattern of its activities, and would put those few women in a very difficult position. It was not thought desirable either for the atmosphere of the institution or for the evaluation design to admit women on a different standard from that applied to men. Of course, if different selection criteria were applied to men and women alike, such as merely serving a term of from one to three years for any crime, which would produce a more substantial number of women in any institution having the broad philosophy and program of the model institution, then much advantage would flow from the inclusion of women offenders. In the last resort, the point is a statistical one; it is dysfunctional to have only a token presence of women prisoners.

3. *Intake and Release Procedures*

From the available pool of prisoners in the state institutions meeting the selection criteria for the proposed institution, a group will be randomly selected to fill the available spaces in the new institution. The prisoner will not be consulted about transfer to this institution; he will be compulsorily transferred. On transfer his first likely parole date will be known, since it is one of the criteria of the selection, but otherwise he will come as does any other prisoner transferred in a prison setting, accompanied by personal and criminal records and by prison records of more or less precision.

The first four to six weeks will be a period of intense and concentrated work with the new prisoner. On arrival he will immediately be assigned to one of the small living groups of

six to eight prisoners which make up an essential part of the
pattern of life of the institution, and he will be integrated as
fully as possible into the normal life of the institution. These
early weeks are also the period when he will be most intensively
interviewed by the staff of the institution. The purpose of these
intensive weeks of intake procedure is to acquaint the prisoner
as precisely as possible with the regimen of the institution, and
in the light of all of the information about him and his crime,
his psychological and sociological circumstances, and a lengthy
and detailed anamnestic discussion with him, to settle with the
prisoner the date of his first furlough from the institution, his
first seventy-two-hour home leave, the date of his first work release from the institution (if a job can be found for him), the
date of his first pre-release placement in a hostel or similar
residential facility in the community (or in his own home, if
he has one), and, most important, the precise date of his parole.
All these tentative decisions will be recorded and the record
made available to the prisoner. He must, if possible, be made
to understand the basis for all these decisions. He will be consulted on them at great length but the decisions will be imposed
on him; he can make only advisory comments and this must
be made absolutely clear to him. By contrast, the more he can
understand, though not necessarily agree to, of the basis of
these decisions the better. There should be no hesitation in con-
fessing to him that such decisions will sometimes be influenced
by actual and anticipated political and community reactions to
him, his crime, and his release.

Setting the individual's parole date months and even years
before he would otherwise be eligible to go to the board is
clearly a major departure from present practice; its justification was offered in the second chapter. Parole board representatives must be brought in at the planning stages of the institution
as coordination with them will be critical.

What is in effect being developed in these early weeks is a
graduated release plan. It is of fundamental importance that
the prisoner's involvement in any treatment program in the
institution must never be made part of the conditions of this
graduated release plan. There is one exception to this. He must
understand that if he stays in the institution he must remain
part of the small living and discussion group to which he has

been allocated. That fact will, of course, be an obvious and unavoidable issue for discussion with the prisoner by the small group in the early days of his intake procedure since on the day of his arrival he will become a part of such a group. It will be one task of the small group of prisoners and staff, as best they can, to give the new potential member of this prison community some understanding of the realities of life in that community.

Within four to six weeks of his arrival there will come the time when the issue must be decided whether the prisoner wishes to stay or not. The aim is to attract "volunteers" to this institution, and that can only be achieved if there are no negative consequences of the prisoner's decision to return to other institutions within the state prison system. It must therefore be possible to arrange his transfer out of the model prison without any negative consequences for his placement in other institutions being drawn from that fact. This is of importance and difficulty, because it must be recognized that there are other institutions within most developing prison systems offering a relatively relaxed and permissive milieu to prisoners, certainly as they approach the last year or two of their sentences. By practice it must be demonstrated that prisoners may reject this new institution and yet not suffer thereby in terms of later disadvantageous placements elsewhere. And, of course, such prisoners carry their parole dates away with them.

These first four to six weeks should give the prisoner ample opportunity to test what resources of self-development are available to him if he wishes to stay in the institution. He should be able to come to understand by personal experience and by the regular small group discussions what this institution could mean to him if he wished to use it. There comes the date when he must decide; and if he decides to stay what has in effect been achieved is his acceptance of a treatment contract. But it is a treatment contract which has the jurisprudentially unusual features that educational and vocational training, psychological self-understanding, and personality developing programs are all entirely facilitative and in no way coerced. He can be in the institution and can be guaranteed his graduated release opportunities entirely independently of participation in any program other than involvement in the small group discussions. This is the central feature of the proposed institution; it constitutes a liberation of the psychological and self-development educative and treatment opportunities from the crippling coercion that has characterized their functioning in other prison settings and implements many of the principles offered earlier in this book. Further, it tends to make correctional processes more rational to the inmate and to stress his creative autonomy and responsibility as a member of a group.

Some problems in this contractual arrangement merit mention. One invariable condition of the institution's adherence to the tentative release dates which have been negotiated will be the prisoner's avoidance of any unjustified physical violence while in the institution. Particularly in this prison, unjustified threatened or actual physical assaults are intolerable. Minor disciplinary matters should not be made part of the graduated release plan; there should be the possibility of the manipulation of other less significant privileges to control less serious disciplinary offenses; but it should be made quite clear that major disciplinary problems will lead to a redefinition of the graduated release plan. In effect, it will be open for renegotiation. And that is an understatement of the situation. What the prisoner must see is that just as he can, at the end of the intake procedure or at any time thereafter, reject the institution, so at any time during the period that he spends in the institution, the institution can for cause shown reject him and send him back to any of the other institutions elsewhere in the prison system. Since such drastic consequences follow the commission of a serious disciplinary offense, it is most important that fair and explicit standards and procedures for disciplinary hearings be established and fully explained to the inmate during the contract negotiation period. Return to the general prison population on these grounds does not mean that the prisoner necessarily loses his parole date; that is an issue to be determined under rules applicable to all prisoners in the relevant state under principles that were discussed in the second chapter.

The environment within the new institution will be as free and permissive as possible; but it will in no wise be permissive of physical violence, or of other major disciplinary problems. It is an institution which aims to run overtly, as well as implicitly, by the consent of all who work in it, staff and prisoners alike.

The theme is to try to carry out the long-established belief that self-regeneration requires that the prisoner hold the key to his own prison. But that key is not his agreement to our view of a treatment program suitable to his self-development or better self-understanding. It is the simple proposition that we will gradually test his capacity to live without crime, particularly violent crime, first in the institutional setting and then more gradually by testing his fitness for a life in the community.

Reception and diagnostic processes on intake into the institution can thus be used for two purposes: First, for purposes of settling the release understanding, to which we have referred. Second, for purposes of lengthy discussions with the prisoner as to the treatment program which may be of assistance to him. Here, with the exception of participation in the small group, the prisoner is both a participant and an equal agent in a true agreement. Release "agreements" are hardly agreements at all, they are explained impositions; but treatment agreements are thereby liberated to be true agreements. Those running the institution know what resources by way of educational, vocational, and psychological treatment they have available. In detailed and lengthy discussion with the prisoner the possibility that these resources may be of use to him will be discussed. Involvement in these programs, as has been stressed and must be stressed to the prisoner, will not be relevant at all to the plans for his gradual release; on the other hand, the thought will cautiously be expressed that it seems to those running the institution somewhat more likely that he will manage to stay out of prison if he is involved in these programs than if he is not.

What if an individual decides at the end of the six weeks' period to stay at the new institution but later changes his mind and asks to be transferred? We cannot justify compelling him to stay in the institution against his wishes in light of our intention to create an environment wherein individuals so motivated can pursue self-change under no compulsion. However, we will require that the inmate desiring to leave give ten to fourteen days' notice in order that arrangements can be made with an appropriate receiving institution within the department.

Furthermore, his decision will become a subject for discussion within his living group. It has been the experience at Grendon Underwood in England, where inmates are permitted to request transfers, that a short cooling off period and the influence of the other inmates in the individual's living unit are quite frequently effective in persuading him to stay.

In a sense both in the initial decision whether to accept transfer to the institution after the introductory period and in this decision whether to remain we are simply shifting the source of coercion to stay from the prison administration to the inmate's small living group. We hope and expect that strong peer pressure will be exerted to keep him at the institution. Of course, this cuts to some degree into the "voluntariness" of these decisions, but we feel that elimination of the normal administrative coercion substantially betters the inmate's position as it allows him to make the decision with the help of those who live and work most closely with him. He will be required to hear their advice but in the end he is free to reject it. And all of us, in prison and out, are subject to varieties of coercion like this.

As has been seen, agreements about graduated release are essential to intake processes, and it may be appropriate to discuss release, somewhat paradoxically, prior to discussion of the treatment program. As the prisoner moves beyond the "probationary" few weeks into his life in the new institution he will know when his first opportunity for a furlough will come. He will be involved in small group discussions with others, about problems that have been met and handled on furloughs by them. He will already know what special provisions have been made limiting the conditions of his first home leave. Perhaps the first leave from the institution will be with a member of the staff for a day's outing or for dinner. This practice, applied at Herstedvester, should be adopted in the model institution. One invariable condition of a seventy-two-hour home leave (which will be given within the first year or the first half of the period before his parole release date, whichever comes first) will, of course, be his avoidance of the commission of a crime while on such a leave, but it may be necessary in many cases to go beyond this. It will normally be necessary to define with precision where he may spend his first home leave. Given the realities of his past life and record it may be necessary to prescribe other more restrictive conditions than this.

An example of some further restrictive conditions may assist. Assume that the prisoner's criminal record reveals a close relationship between excessive drinking and the commission of crimes of violence. It may be necessary for the institutional authorities to say to him that he may go on furlough, or on work release, or on pre-release placement, if, but only if, he does not drink. In such circumstances it should be made clear to him that the authorities will take pains to investigate whether he does indeed drink while on furlough or pre-release placement, and that to achieve this purpose they will not hesitate to use any constitutionally available investigative resources.

This group of offenders has to learn to live with a sometimes harassing police force, and it is a sound idea to use the police not infrequently to check up on their adherence to trial release conditions. And, of course, to tell the prisoner that this will be done.

A word should be added about work or educational release to a halfway house. Continuity of treatment is a cornerstone of this whole plan. Graduates of the model institution will have their own halfway house—an apartment or small townhouse will be adequate. Before the individual is paroled or if, when paroled, he has nowhere to live, he will have the opportunity to spend several months at the halfway house. The staff of the model prison will be responsible for the halfway house, as well, and will maintain relations with the inmate during this period.

I am recommending here the practice of Maryland's Patuxent Institute, where the individual staff members who work closely with a prisoner at Patuxent are also his parole agents. They meet with him at the halfway house, generally in small group evening meetings, once a week in the first months after parole and with reduced frequency thereafter. Because the institution is small the case loads should not be overly burdensome.

In sum, the release conditions that should be attached to all forms of graduated testing of larger increments of freedom, which is the principle that is being manipulated, are the avoidance of crime and the avoidance of proscribed behavioral patterns that have been found to be closely related to the offender's criminal behavior in the past or to the political feasibility of continuing him on the graduated release program. If release is approached in this light it has an enormously liberating effect on the possibility of planning and carrying out a voluntary treatment program.

4. Staff Selection and Training

Inadequately trained and poorly motivated staff is a chronic prison problem. In maximum security prisons, staff turnover remains so high that continuities in programming become impossible. In addition, many so-called "rehabilitative" institutions evidence impregnable divisions between administrative, security, and treatment staffs that preclude creation of an environment facilitative of self-change.

It is clear that the proposed model institution will stand or fall on the quality of its staff. Does this mean that unusually highly trained and experienced staff must be selected to work in the institution? By no means. The whole institution must be seen as an innovative experiment in self-development and self-training efforts, and that means for prisoners and staff alike. A small clinical professionally trained staff of four or five will play their largest roles in the intake procedure, in negotiating the graduated release contract, in handling crises or assisting in handling crises in the institution, and in running a continuous staff training program which uses as its study material the day-to-day life of the institution. Other nonclinical professionals (lawyers and sociologists, for example) should be recruited to top administrative positions and be held responsible for coordinating a balanced treatment program. The linchpin of that program is the front-of-the-line staff member involved in the small group discussions, or working in the educational or vocational programs, or in the workshops or on the playing fields.

Inadequate salaries are, of course, one reason for poor morale and large turnover, but a thorough study of citizen attitudes toward various jobs in the criminal justice system has shown more concern among high school students that "guards can't do anything" than with their poor pay in explaining lack of preference for this kind of work. Prison work should be better paid and salaries are increasing; but it is unlikely to become highly remunerative. This should not be seen as an impossible obstacle to creating a model prison. After all, many talented individuals in our society are drawn to less remunerative work than they could otherwise obtain when they feel that the work is both particularly valuable to the community and self-fulfilling. What needs to be offered to the potential and recruited staff for this institution is a chance to contribute substantially to a challenging social experiment.

There is a need to redefine the role of line personnel in prison work if we are to upgrade their self-esteem and hence their morale. The Task Force on Corrections of the President's Commission spoke of a new kind of "collaborative" institution where all staff members are integrated into the primary rehabilitative tasks of the institution. Developing a truly collaborative institution will be a major challenge in the institution for the repetitively violent. The American Correctional Association's Joint Commission on Correctional Manpower and Training was wise in suggesting that determined efforts should be made to recruit members of minorities and women to this work. Ex-prisoners should also be employed.

Narrowing the racial and cultural chasm that today separates staff and prisoners would increase communication between these castes and might suggest role models for some prisoners. Putting aside secretarial and administrative support personnel, it seems likely that a staff of about 150 would be required to run the proposed institution. Ideally, staffing should be higher than this, but such is the parsimony of staffing of correctional institutions in this country that more is unlikely to be achieved. The figure of 150 is, of course, subject to debate and negotiation; it is offered only as an initial estimate. Of these 150 staff, 40 percent to 50 percent should be women and, further, minorities should be represented among the staff at all levels of seniority and training in roughly the same distribution as in the prisoner population. Given the realities of the American criminal justice system this would mean a disproportionate number of blacks and other minorities.

That the injection of women into the prison at all levels, including that of front-of-the-line-guard, will tend to reduce violence is offered as a confident proposition; it is certainly timely to test it. As a matter of observation, men behave better in the presence of women. The social skills of many male offenders in dealing with women are distorted and undeveloped. Frequent and constructive association with women as staff members of the prison will have a positive impact upon the prisoners' later social relationships. Of course, it need hardly be noted that front-line work in a maximum security prison is not the kind of work that will be attractive to a majority of women (or men, for that matter) or for which a majority will be suited. Women recruits will need to be made sensitive to the problems of sexual anxieties that are noticeable in many individuals who have been incarcerated for a long period of time. Fears of sexual inadequacy and hence of sexual readjustment upon release are substantial in prison. Not only younger women should be recruited; the work is suitable for more mature women also and mothers and other women coming back into the work force should be included. In view of the matriarchal nature of the black family and the generally idealized view of the mother in both black and Latino subcultures, minority women in the forty-plus age group should be particularly sought after.

Recent recruitment of ex-offenders and ex-prisoners into corrections in many states is a development to be emulated in the model prison. The creation of career opportunities in corrections for ex-prisoners not only affords an excellent rehabilitation technique for them but allows them to demonstrate that some prisoners do indeed "make it," in sharp contrast to the depressing presence of ex-prisoner recidivists who will be in abundant supply in this as in other prisons. The numbers of ex-prisoners on the staff need not be large; but applicants with criminal records certainly should not be rejected.

Just as the life of the prisoner within the institution will be characterized by many small group meetings, so the life for the staff member should be characterized by a high level of involvement in discussion with other members of the staff on the day-to-day life of the institution, and on particular problems faced by particular inmates. A professional orientation toward the job must be cultivated. There must be frequent staff meetings, bringing together staff members from every level of the institution. However, when the problems of a particular prisoner are discussed, or the problems which he presents to the prison are discussed, whenever possible that prisoner should be brought in to the discussion and should be freely allowed to take the discussion material back to his own small prisoner and staff discussion group. The overall effort is to run an autonomous community, perceptive of the peculiar difficulties of its membership.

All staff should be encouraged to participate in their off-duty hours in any of the programs that are available to inmates. It is a training and self-development institution for them too if they wish it to be. One of its express functions should be to train staff members to take greater and greater responsibilities and so to open opportunities for them at higher levels in the Department of Corrections and in other career lines.

It is clear that in developing such a total therapeutic yet uncoervice milieu the role of the first director and of his supportive staff is of first importance. The small groups which lie at the core of the institutional program have, in effect, a perpetual life. Their influence should develop and grow independent of particular prisoner or staff membership, yet be influenced by all who pass through them. The director and the nucleus of his supporting clinical staff should be appointed at least a year before the first prisoner is transferred for intake procedure. The prison should start small and grow gradually. Let us envisage a staff of, say, twenty beyond the clinical staff, to begin with, and an early intake of no more than thirty prisoners, and that gradually. The aim is to begin slowly to evolve the milieu of the institution, to form the small discussion groups which on a daily basis thrash out the myriad growing problems that the institution will face. Gradually new small groups will be formed out of the earlier groups; the culture should grow, the pattern of life of the institution evolve.

Initial recruitment should be of some staff with little experience in prison work as well as some who have worked with inmates but who are flexible enough to adapt to the new concepts of staff roles at this prison. Thereafter, when the life of the institution takes on shape and continuity, it should be possible to make work in this institution an available option for those in the prison service generally who would like to try their hand.

A brief training program will be a necessary stage in staff intake; but more reliance will be placed on supervised on-the-job training than on classroom presentations. Part of the initial introduction to the institution, such as presentations by different staff members in which they explain their functions and the programs they operate, should be offered at the same time to new staff and new inmates. Training for staff should emphasize the type of interpersonal skills which support the overall philosophy of the prison and should help them to avoid the traditional keeper or turnkey role that characterizes their work in most prisons.

If the model prison is to succeed it must be a place in which the staff can grow along decent career lines of opportunity for their own self-development and self-advancement, at least to the same extent that is available to prisoners. Therefore, it should not be seen as necessarily desirable to have many staff working in the institution who have been there for many years. If the institution is to succeed for prisoners it should also succeed for staff, which means that they should grow to positions of larger responsibility in the prison service or elsewhere. Just as this new institution will be more demanding as well as more free for prisoners, so it will be very much more demanding for the staff who work in it; this should be recognized and opportunities for advancement should be available based on that recognition.

As to the senior staff of the institution: The director and the two top assistants should, as was suggested, be appointed at least a year before the opening of the model prison. They must become acquainted with recent penological literature, visit prisons in this country, in Canada and in Europe, wherever innovative efforts are being made to treat violent offenders, and involve themselves deeply in planning for the evolution of the model institution and in recruiting its staff.

Much thought should be given to the qualities and background desired in the first director, warden, or superintendent, both in terms of the skills and personal qualities needed and the expectations which inmates, staff, and the general public will form in the light of his or her professional background. The tendency for institutions with psychiatrists and clinical psychologists at the head to be associated in the public's mind with mental hospitals is unfortunate, and the stigmatizing effect of this on the prison should not be underestimated. On the other hand, clinical staff will play a major role in the model prison. Whether a psychiatrist or a clinical psychologist should be the chief administrator or rather be number two man or woman in charge of clinical programs is a question of difficulty and importance. A figure from a neutral area, like law or business, might be considered as the first incumbent; this might help to avoid the dangerous schisms that often develop between professional "treaters" and others in the prison service. Personal skills and attitudes rather than professional identity should, however, be the deciding factor.

In addition to the chief administrator and a senior clinician in psychology or psychiatry, it will be necessary to recruit three or four other professionally trained persons with clinical backgrounds in psychology or social work. Responsibility for treating individual prisoners and for supervising and training other staff members, both within the model prison and in the special after-care facilities, will fall on this small clinical staff, and the quality of their work in the early formative years of the institution's life will be of particular importance.

5. *Institutional Program and Living Units*

This is the heart of the matter, yet it can be treated relatively briefly. The operational structure so far suggested for this model prison for repetitively violent criminals has set it free to offer any and all treatment modalities, substantially unimpeded by the effects of coercion, hypocrisy, and condescension that have tended to corrupt other rehabilitative efforts in prisons. The matter was discussed as an issue of principle in the second chapter; its practical fulfillment requires only brief commentary.

The goal of this institution will be to help its inmates live without crime upon release, especially without violent crime, should they decide to try to do so. The overall program of the prison will be directed to developing a milieu conducive to that end. It will include treatment modalities—educative, vocational, clinical, and recreational—all on a voluntary basis. Only two aspects of the prison program will be obligatory. Every prisoner must participate in a small "living group" and he must fulfill his assigned stint in the daily work program.

All existing treatment programs within penal institutions that are thought worthy of emulation can be made available in the model prison, if funds and trained staff can be found. Some treatment modalities are suited to provision on a contract basis with those providing such treatments on the outside; to some, such as certain college courses, suitable prisoners will go out from the prison on a daily basis. Others will be intramural and provided by the prison staff. The range should be great, from literacy training to plastic surgery. And it merits repetition that this wide range of educational and treatment modalities should be introduced to the inmate as his awareness of his needs and wants increases and as he and the staff agree on the likelihood of any particular program being helpful to him. If he is illiterate, it must be entirely his decision whether he wishes to remain so or not. If he lacks a trade, he must be free to leave the prison with that lack. After all, the reason the institution is to be established is not for remedial education but because the community sees in it a means of banishing those who behave in an intolerable fashion and of fulfilling a faint hope that they might not, when they return, reengage in that behavior. That is the central reason for the assumption of power over the prisoner, and that fact must limit the coercive quality of any of our responses to him. The one exception to this principle of the substitution of the facilitation of change for an attempt to coerce cure is that certain rules which were negotiated at the time of intake remain part of the obligatory milieu of the institution, namely, his avoidance of any physical violence and his participation in a small group living experience.

If the prisoner is set free to develop his capacity to avoid violent crime in the future, this is likely to come less from the formal treatment programs than from the total milieu of the institution, and from the crucial small group discussions involving other prisoners and the staff. In these discussions, the prisoner with his fellow prisoners and staff will probe the lessons of the many ordinary human encounters which take place daily within the institution and on temporary absences from the institution.

The small living groups should consist of six to eight inmates and two to four staff members who share meals and discussions before and after the normal working day, every day, six days a week. The staff members will not be professional clinical staff but front-line staff, men or women working in the institution. The prisoner and staff group should also send representatives to a variety of committees whose work will be of importance to the life of the institution as a whole—a self-government committee, an institutional program committee, a discipline committee, committees on entertainment and recreation, and so on.

The organization of the small living groups should be directed toward an intense concern with their responsibilities to one another, with an examination of their crimes, the harm caused, and with the possibilities of a reconciliation with themselves and their victim or victim's family. Leadership of the group will be by the staff, but should be shared with the prisoners in terms of agenda and the intensity of examination of any particular prisoner's problems.

During the initial four to six weeks of stay the prisoner will join with his small living group in an intensive period of examination of the milieu, of himself, and of the requirements as well as the expectations of his future in the prison. In addition to discussion with his small group, the prisoner will have daily opportunities to speak and to write about himself with a single staff member assigned to him from his group. Out of these encounters will come the data that the offender may use to decide whether he wishes to remain and participate in the institutional program and, if he decides to stay, to prepare with the staff an individualized plan for his participation and treatment for the remainder of his stay in the institution. As the crucial decision week approaches, the prisoner's anxiety level will increase, providing additional data to the staff and the prisoner himself regarding treatment planning.

The small group experience should help the inmate establish new behavior patterns and new methods of adapting to life situations. The material for discussion at the small group meetings will encompass everything in the daily life of the institution and of the members of the group—prisoners and staff. Group work is immensely enriched by the fact that the members of each group are at different stages of their prison experience. At any one time in each such group there will be one or two recent arrivals, one or two approaching their first furlough or returning from furloughs, one or two "working out" or "studying out" from the institution, one or two beginning to face the promise and challenge of placement in a pre-parole hostel or of parole. The panorama of the life and progression of the institution and of each of its inmates should be captured in every small living group.

Weekly staff meetings should be scheduled at which one or two particular prisoners are discussed. The prisoner being discussed should generally be allowed to attend and to participate. This meeting would be for all staff and would provide opportunities for learning, modifying treatment plans, and examining staff attitudes or behavior which might interfere with the prisoner's progress. The staff would also have frequent regularly scheduled meetings among themselves for formal education and training, discussion and task-oriented problem solving.

As well as academic, vocational, and recreational programs being available to the prisoner, there is need for some specialized medical, psychiatric, and psychological services. Such therapy opportunities may be individualized or offered in groups of various sizes. Larger groups for psychotherapy, say up to twenty-four participants, are more economical and there is evidence that they are as effective as smaller groups and one-to-one psychotherapy in treating many prisoners' violent behavior.

Drugs and medication should be used at the institution only when the suffering of the prisoner indicates a serious danger of psychological decomposition or when medication is necessary to diminish an emotional state such as anxiety to the point where the individual is able to participate in institutional life. Even in these instances, medication should be used sparingly since an important treatment goal is to help the individual live with and control his anxieties without depending on medication.

Educational, vocational training and treatment programs should normally take place after normal working hours. We are dealing with an adult group and only in special circumstances should arrangements be made for school or college work to be done as part of the ordinary work program. There are occasions when this is appropriate, calling for daily educational release to go to nearby schools or colleges, but the general pattern of life within the institution should be as similar as possible to the ordinary working life of a citizen in the community.

Whereas participation in the work program of the prison, its industries and its maintenance, is properly required of every inmate, there is a difficult problem of the quality and duration of work that should be provided. It is desirable to provide for the prisoner as near as ordinary vocational and industrial opportunities as exist outside; on the other hand, to do so will be to make this prison very different from most other prisons which face intractable problems in prison labor. Outmoded machinery, a lack of available industries, pervading idleness, make-work, maintenance in lieu of work, a pittance instead of a wage, all plague most American prisons. Should this new institution seek to provide its inmates a regular, busy working day at useful industries? To do so would complicate the task of evaluating the consequences of this change in relation to other changes in the model prison's program and philosophy.

The preferences of the research methodologist must yield to the need to make this a model institution. It is unwise to be too precious in one's approach to the difficult task of creating a humane and crime-preventing prison; our overall experience with prisons has not been encouraging; we should not limit our efforts to make a creative milieu in any new institution. Nor are the methodological problems insuperable. Provided the total package of what is done in the new institution can be repeated without undue cost in other institutions, the first round of evaluative effort of the total package is worthwhile; refinements can wait.

A program of useful work should be established at the prison, not as a treatment program, but simply because this is regarded in our society as a substantial part of the life of the ordinary adult. There is no good reason that inmates should be exempted from this responsibility. By the same token, inmates in the work program should be compensated at a rate competitive with that paid for similar work on the outside and should return part of their salary for room and board. Those permitted educational leave in lieu of daytime work should be similarly compensated.

The general design, then, is that treatment of repetitively violent prisoners take place in a humane and secure setting, in which the prisoner has knowledge of his release date and of a graduated release program. Therapies are deployed as prisoner and staff work together to develop a voluntary treatment plan for each prisoner. The setting and participation in it offer the prisoner a relatively stable environment in which he is less fearful and therefore can use energies to examine his own fears, impulses, and crimes in a way which gives him a sense of control over himself and his behavior and in which he can develop confidence in his relationships within a small group, his social roles, and his work. He experiences increments of freedom and of responsibility which test his capacity to tolerate stress and help him to react without violence to troublesome environmental pressures and personal stimuli which previously precipitated his criminal violence.

6. *Evaluation*

The staff which spent a year planning the institution described in this chapter gave extended attention to the crucial problem of evaluating this prison, deciding what if anything it is good for and why, discovering with which categories of offenders it may be effective and for whom it might be unhelpful or injurious. A careful research design emerged which is available to the interested scholar or administrator; there is no need to burden this chapter with the details. But a few principles of an effective evaluation of the proposed model institution merit mention.

A diagrammatic survey of the evaluation design is helpful (fig. 1). It is related to Illinois statistics since those were under consideration by the planning staff. This diagram accepts the "black box" view of evaluation of this institution and places no great reliance on factor analysis or on measuring treatment impacts on subgroups of the treated population, certainly in the first phase of evaluative efforts. Later, the institution's impact on subgroups of the T group and further stratification of the pool from which "volunteers" are selected should be pursued.

By distinguishing between the C_1 and C_2 groups, providing for the C_2 group the intensive after-care that will be given to

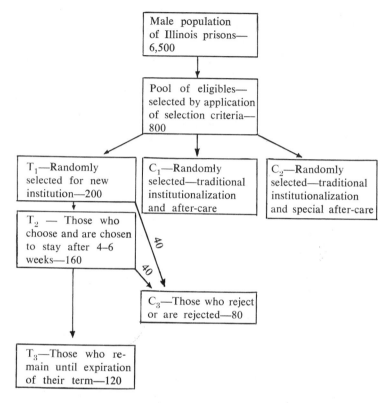

Fig. 1. C_1, C_2, and C_3 will be further broken down according to the institutions to which they are assigned so that comparisons can be made between various T groups and those in C groups in different institutions.

all T groups, an effort is made to tease out the impact this part of the treatment program makes on the overall program.

The primary aim of this institution is to help its inmates live without further violent crime upon release. Thus the principal purpose of the evaluation design is to build into the institution techniques for determining whether the overall effect of the new institution has been to reduce the incidence and severity of later violence of those selected to be sent there as compared to inmates of similar ages and with similar records who remain in the general prison population. At some point after the institution has been established and a number of its graduates have been in the free community long enough for their capacity to live without violent crime to be tested, it must be possible for an independent evaluator to report that the institution has failed to accomplish this goal, if that is the case. Unless there is this possibility for disproof of the institution based on a rigorous objective evaluation design there is no real possibility for scientifically establishing its success.

Of course, reducing recidivism is by no means the only goal of the proposed institution. It is likely, for example, that it will have a beneficial effect on other aspects of the inmate's life upon release, such as job stability and personal relationships; that the inmate's time in the institution will be less damaging; and that the attitudes and career patterns of staff will be improved. Measurement of the achievement of these and other legitimate goals of the institution must be included in the evaluation design. Nevertheless, unless the later violent crime of the test group is less than (or at least no greater than) that of the control group, the institution must be determined a failure and its design abandoned for other approaches to dealing with repetitively violent offenders.

The selection procedure has been designed to create the different test (T) and control (C) groups outlined in the diagram, which can be compared in a number of different ways to evaluate different aspects of the impact of the new institution. The first step is to apply the criteria developed earlier in this chapter to the male population of state penal institutions. All of the selection criteria must be applied at this point so that assignment to the test and control groups will be truly random. Otherwise there is the danger that once it is known whether an individual is in the test or control group, intentionally or not such criteria would be unevenly applied.

When the initial pool of eligible inmates is determined, the average age and age distribution should be compared with the general prison population. If the pool is significantly older or has a markedly different age distribution, the age selection criteria must be revised or the sample randomly adjusted to correct this; otherwise the applicability to the general prison population of whatever success this institution achieves is unnecessarily limited.

Let us assume that application of the selection criteria to the present Illinois male prison population yields eight hundred inmates. From this group a predetermined number will be randomly selected to be sent to the new institution (T_1) or to be the control group (C_1) which will continue on the traditional course through the existing Illinois institutions. Again for the sake of discussion assume that two hundred individuals are assigned to each group.* Comparison of these two groups will reflect the impact of the new institution on the prison system and will produce hard data capable of being reproduced. For the institution to continue T_1 must do at least as well according to the relevant criteria as C_1.

Note that there is an important subgroup (C_3) within T_1—those who reject the new institution at the end of the initiation period plus those who initially decide to stay but later request a transfer or after violation of their contract conditions are compulsorily transferred back to the general prison population. At first glance it may seem unfair to saddle the institution's measurement of success with individuals who do not complete or even enter its program. Only by including this entire group, however, can we maintain the integrity of the randomized sample. Only by this method is the impact of the total intervention on the system measured (Glaser, 1973, p. 71). Furthermore, unless the C_3 group is included in T_1, any success of the institution could be attributed to the difference between those who volunteer and abide by their contract and those who do not, rather than to the effect of the institution's program.

As with all ongoing people-changing experiments, there is the evaluation problem that both the model prison and the test groups will change over time. At any point the evaluation will reflect only the effect of the prison as it operated several years earlier on the group of prisoners who then experienced its program. There is no solution to this; only the palliative that it is necessary to continue evaluative work permanently as a part of

*Actually the number initially sent to the new institution will be much less since the plan is to begin with a small group and expand gradually as the milieu is established. Also for an institution with a maximum capacity of 200, probably something like 120 or 130 will be assigned directly from the pool since space must be reserved for graduates who are returned for parole violations or crimes committed after release.

policy and program planning and that the model can be duplicated in a variety of settings.

The proposed prison should be evaluated on the basis of five broad criteria: the prisoner's behavior in the community after release, the cost of the new institution, its humaneness, its effect on the rest of the system, and its effect on staff attitudes and careers. How these categories of measurement and their components are weighed is essentially a public policy and political question. Little assistance can be offered, for example, on the question of how many dollars per inmate per year the system should be willing to spend to create a specific level of humaneness and decency of treatment for this type of prisoner at the new institution. All that is suggested is that each of these criteria of assessment is relevant and important in any judgment of the social value of this model.

As already discussed, the most important test of the new institution will be the recidivism rate of its group as compared with that of the control group. Although data should be collected for all parole revocations, arrests, and convictions of the test and control groups, the significant data for determining whether the institution should continue is that pertaining to convictions for violent crimes. Violations should be analyzed by seriousness, frequency, and time at large before the new crime was committed.

A final, perhaps obvious, point. The evaluation team must be independent of the administration of the institution. There is, in evaluative correctional research a history of subtle and sometimes not so subtle pressures which have tended to produce a depressing correlation between who does the research and what the research finds. Such pressures must neither corrupt nor appear to corrupt the critical testing of this model.

Selected Reading and References

Alexander, Meryl E. *Jail Administration.* Springfield, Ill.: Thomas, 1957.

Allen, Francis A. *The Borderland of Criminal Justice: Essays in Law and Criminology.* Chicago: University of Chicago Press, 1964.

————. *The Crimes of Politics.* Cambridge, Mass.: Harvard University Press, 1974.

Alper, Benedict S., and Boren, Jerry F. *Crime: International Agenda: Concern and Action in the Prevention of Crime and Treatment of Offenders, 1846–1972.* Lexington, Mass.: D. C. Heath, 1972.

Alschuler, Albert W. "The Prosecutor's Role in Plea Bargaining." *University of Chicago Law Review* 36 (1968): 50–112.

American Assembly, Columbia University. *Prisoners in America.* Edited by Lloyd E. Ohlin. Englewood Cliffs, N.J.: Prentice-Hall, 1973.

————. *Report of the Forty-second American Assembly, December 17–20, 1972, Arden House, Harriman, New York: Prisoners in America.* New York: American Assembly, Columbia University, 1973.

American Bar Association Project on Minimum Standards for Criminal Justice. *Standards Relating to Appellate Review of Sentences, Approved Draft.* New York: American Bar Association, Office of Criminal Justice Project, Institute of Judicial Administration, 1968.

123

————. *Standards Relating to Pleas of Guilty, Approved Draft.* New York: American Bar Association, Office of Criminal Justice Project, Institute of Judicial Administration, 1968.

————. *Standards Relating to Sentencing Alternatives and Procedures, Approved Draft.* New York: American Bar Association, Office of Criminal Justice Project, Institute of Judicial Administration, 1968.

American Correctional Association Parole Corrections Project. *Resource Document No. 3: The Mutual Agreement Program, a Planned Change in Correctional Service Delivery.* College Park, Md.: American Correctional Association, 1973.

American Friends Service Committee. *Struggle for Justice: A Report on Crime and Punishment in America.* New York: Hill & Wang, 1971.

American Law Institute. *A Model Code of Pre-Arraignment Procedure, Tentative Draft No. 5.* Philadelphia: American Law Institute, 1972.

————. *Model Penal Code: Proposed Official Draft.* Philadelphia: American Law Institute, 1962.

Ancel, Marc: "Principal Aspects of Modern European Penology." *Proceedings of the American Philosophical Society* 118 (1974): 254–59.

————. *Social Defence: A Modern Approach to Criminal Problems.* Translated by J. Wilson. New York: Schocken Books, 1966.

Andenaes, Johannes. *Punishment and Deterrence.* Ann Arbor: University of Michigan Press, 1974.

Barnes, Harry Elmer. *The Evolution of Penology in Pennsylvania: A Study in American Social History.* Indianapolis: Bobbs-Merrill, 1927.

Barry, John Vincent. *Alexander Maconochie of Norfolk Island: A Study of a Pioneer in Penal Reform.* Melbourne: Oxford University Press, 1958.

Beaumont, Gustave de, and Tocqueville, Alexis de. *On The Penitentiary System in the United States and Its Application in France.* Translated by Francis Lieber. Introduction by Thorsten Sellin. Perspectives in Sociology Series, edited by Herman R. Lantz. Carbondale, Ill.: Southern Illinois University Press, 1964. First published in Philadelphia by Carey, Lea & Blanchard, 1833.

Beccaria, Cesare. *Dei delitti e delle pene.* Leghorn, Italy: Aubert, 1764. The first English translation was *An Essay on Crimes and Punishments.* London: J. Almon, 1767. For a more recent translation see Beccaria, Cesare. *On Crimes and Punishments.* Translated by Henry Paolucci. Indianapolis: Bobbs-Merrill, 1963. See too: Maestro, Marcello. *Cesare Beccaria and the Origins of Penal Reform.* Philadelphia: Temple University Press, 1973.

Behan, Brendan. *Borstal Boy.* New York: Alfred A. Knopf, 1959.

Bixby, F. Lovell. "A New Role for Parole Boards." *Federal Probation* 34 (June 1970): 24–28.

————. "A Working Plan for the Individualized Institutional Training of Offenders." Paper presented at the 60th Annual Congress of the American Prison Association, Louisville, Kentucky, October 16, 1930.

Blumstein, Alfred, and Cohen, Jacqueline. "A Theory of the Stability of Punishment." *Journal of Criminal Law and Criminology* 64 (1973): 198–207.

Boorstin, Daniel Joseph. *The Americans: The Democratic Experience.* New York: Random House, 1973.

Burgess, Anthony. *A Clockwork Orange.* New York: W. W. Norton, 1963.

Burt, Robert A. "Biotechnology and Anti-Social Conduct: Controlling the Controllers." *The Ohio State Law Forum* Lectures for 1974 delivered at Columbus, Ohio, on April 30 and May 1, 1974.

Cahn, Edmond N. *The Sense of Injustice: An Anthropocentric View of Law.* New York: New York University Press, 1949.

Chambliss, William J. *Crime and the Legal Process.* New York: McGraw-Hill, 1969.

————. "Types of Deviance and the Effectiveness of Legal Sanctions." *Wisconsin Law Review* 1967: 703–19.

Chappell, Duncan and Wilson, Paul. *The Australian Criminal Justice System.* Sydney: Butterworths, 1972.

Christie, Nils. "Changes in Penal Values." In *Scandinavian Studies in Criminology: Aspects of Social Control in Welfare States.* Edited by Nils Christie, 2: 161–72. Oslo: Scandinavian University Books, 1968.

Clark, Ramsey. *Crime in America: Observations on Its Nature, Causes, Prevention and Control.* New York: Simon & Schuster, 1970.

Cleaver, Eldridge. *Soul on Ice.* New York: Dell, 1968.

Clinard, Marshall B., and Quinney, Richard. *Criminal Behavior Systems: A Typology.* New York: Holt, Rinehart and Winston, 1967.

Cohen, Harold L. "Educational Therapy: The Design of Learning Environments." *Research in Psychotherapy: Proceedings of the Third Conference of the American Psychological Association, Chicago, Illinois, May 31–June 4, 1966* 3 (1968): 21–53.

Cohen, Stanley, and Taylor, Laurie. *Psychological Survival: The Experience of Long-Term Imprisonment.* Harmondsworth, England: Penguin, 1972.

Committee for Economic Development. `Reducing Crime and Assuring Justice: A Statement on National Policy by the Research and Policy Committee of the Committee for Economic Development.* New York: Committee for Economic Development, 1972.

Conrad, John P. "Corrections and Simple Justice." *Journal of Criminal Law and Criminology* 64 (1973): 208–17.

————. *Crime and Its Correction: An International Survey of Atti-*

tudes and Practices. Berkeley: University of California Press, 1967.

Council of Judges of the National Council on Crime and Delinquency. *Model Sentencing Act.* 2d ed. Washington, D.C.: National Council on Crime and Delinquency, 1972.

Cramton, Roger C. "Driver Behavior and Legal Sanctions: A Study of Deterrence." *Michigan Law Review* 67 (1969): 421–54.

Cressey, Donald R., ed. *Crime and Criminal Justice.* Chicago: Quadrangle Press, 1971.

Cressey, Donald R., and McDermott, Robert A. *Diversion from the Juvenile Justice System.* Ann Arbor: National Assessment of Juvenile Corrections, University of Michigan, 1973.

Cressey, Donald R., and Ward, David A., eds. *Delinquency, Crime and Social Process.* New York: Harper and Row, 1969.

Cross, A. R. N. *Paradoxes in Prison Sentences: An Inaugural Lecture Delivered before the University of Oxford on 5 March, 1965.* Oxford: Clarendon Press, 1965.

————. *Punishment, Prison and the Public: An Assessment of Penal Reform in Twentieth Century England by an Armchair Penologist.* London: Stevens & Sons, 1971.

Davis, Angela Y.; Magee, Ruchell; the Soledad Brothers; and other Political Prisoners. *If They Come in the Morning.* New York: Signet, 1971.

Davis, Kenneth Culp. *Discretionary Justice.* Baton Rouge: Louisiana State University Press, 1969.

Dawson, Robert O. *Sentencing: The Decision as to Type, Length, and Conditions of Sentence.* Report of the American Bar Foundation's Survey of the Administration of Criminal Justice in the United States, edited by Frank J. Remington. Boston: Little, Brown, 1969.

DePuy, LeRoy B. "The Walnut Street Prison: Pennsylvania's First Penitentiary." *Pennsylvania History: Quarterly Journal of the Pennsylvania Historical Society* 18 (1951):130–44.

Dinitz, Simon, and Reckless, Walter C. *Critical Issues in the Study of Crime.* Boston: Little, Brown, 1968.

Enker, Arnold N. "Perspectives on Plea Bargaining." In President's Commission on Law Enforcement and Administration of Justice. *Task Force Report: The Courts.* Washington, D.C.: U.S. Government Printing Office, 1967.

Ericson, Richard V. *Turning the Inside Out: On Limiting the Use of Imprisonment.* Community Education Series 1, no. 3. Toronto: John Howard Society of Ontario, n.d.

Erikson, Kai T. *Wayward Puritans: A Study in the Sociology of Deviance.* New York: Wiley, 1966.

Ewing, Alfed Cyril. *The Morality of Punishment: With Some Sug-*

gestions for a General Theory of Ethics. London: Kegan Paul, Trench, Trubner & Co., 1929.

Eysenck, Hans Jurgen. *Crime and Personality.* Boston: Houghton Mifflin, 1964.

Feinberg, Joel. *Doing and Deserving: Essays in the Theory of Responsibility.* Princeton: Princeton University Press, 1970.

Frankel, Marvin E. *Criminal Sentences: Law without Order.* New York: Hill and Wang, 1973.

Geis, Gilbert, and Monahan, John. "The Social Ecology of Violence." In *Man and Morality,* edited by T. Lickona. New York: Holt, Rinehart and Winston, in press.

Gerber, Rudolph H., and McAnany, Patrick D., eds. *Contemporary Punishment: Views, Explanations, and Justifications.* Notre Dame, Ind.: University of Notre Dame Press, 1972.

Glaser, Daniel, ed. *Crime in the City.* New York: Harper and Row, 1970.

————. *The Effectiveness of a Prison and Parole System.* New York: Bobbs-Merrill, 1964.

————. "The Efficacy of Alternative Approaches to Parole Prediction." *American Sociological Review* 20 (1955): 283–87.

————. "Prediction Tables as Accounting Devices for Judges and Parole Boards." *Crime and Delinquency* 8 (1962): 239–58.

————. *Routinizing Evaluation: Getting Feedback on Effectiveness of Crime and Delinquency Programs.* Rockville, Md.: National Institute of Mental Health, Center for Studies of Crime and Delinquency, 1973.

Goffman, Erving. *Asylums.* Garden City, N.Y.: Doubleday, 1961.

Goldfarb, Ronald L., and Singer, Linda R. *After Conviction: A Review of the American Correction System.* New York: Simon and Schuster, 1973.

Goldstein, Joseph; Freud, Anna; and Solnit, Albert J. *Beyond the Best Interest of the Child.* New York: Free Press, 1973.

Gottfredson, Donald. "Assessment and Prediction Methods in Crime and Delinquency." In President's Commission on Law Enforcement and Administration of Justice. *Task Force Report: Juvenile Delinquency and Youth Crime.* Washington, D.C.: U.S. Government Printing Office, 1967.

Gottfredson, Donald, et al. *Four Thousand Lifetimes: A Study of Time Served and Parole Outcomes.* Davis, Calif.: National Council on Crime and Delinquency, Research Center, 1973.

Granucci, Anthony F. " 'Nor Cruel and Unusual Punishments Inflicted': The Original Meaning." *California Law Review* 57 (1969): 839–65.

Gray, William J. "The English Prison Medical Service: Its Historical Background and More Recent Developments." In *Medi-*

cal Care of Prisoners and Detainees. Ciba Foundation Symposium 16. Amsterdam: Associated Scientific Publishers, 1973.

Greenberg, David F. "Rehabilitation Is Still Punishment." In William Adler-Geller, "The Problem of Prisons: A Way Out?" *The Humanist,* May–June, 1972, pp. 24–33.

———. "A Reply [to "A Response to *Struggle for Justice,*" by Edmund B. Spaeth, Jr.]." *Prison Journal* 52 (1972): 33–41.

Grob, Gerald N. "Welfare and Poverty in American History: . . . David J. Rothman, *The Discovery of the Asylum: Social Order and Disorder in the New Republic." Reviews in American History* 1 (1973): 43–52.

Grünhut, Max. *Penal Reform: A Comparative Study.* Oxford: Clarendon Press, 1948.

Hakeem, Michael. "A Critique of the Psychiatric Approach to Crime and Correction." *Law and Contemporary Problems* 23 (1958): 650–82.

Halleck, Seymour, M.D. *The Politics of Therapy.* New York: Science House, 1971.

———. *Psychiatry and the Dilemmas of Crime.* New York: Harper, 1967.

Hart, H. L. A. *Law, Liberty and Morality.* London: Oxford University Press, 1963.

———. *Punishment and Responsibility: Essays in the Philosophy of Law.* London: Oxford University Press, 1968.

———. "Rawls on Liberty and Its Priority." *University of Chicago Law Review* 40 (1973): 534–55.

Harvard Law Review Note. "Developments in the Law: Civil Commitment of the Mentally Ill." *Harvard Law Review* 87 (1974): 1245–53.

Harvard Law Review Note. "The Unconstitutionality of Plea Bargaining." *Harvard Law Review* 83 (1970): 1387–1411.

Haskell, Martin R., and Yablonsky, Lewis. *Crime and Delinquency.* Chicago: Rand McNally, 1970.

Heath, James. *Eighteenth Century Penal Theory.* London: Oxford University Press, 1963.

Henry, Joan. *Women in Prison.* New York: Doubleday, 1952.

Hood, Roger, and Sparks, Richard. *Key Issues in Criminology.* World University Library Series. New York: McGraw-Hill, 1970.

Howard, Derek Lionel. *The English Prisons: Their Past and Their Future.* London: Methuen, 1960.

Howard, John. *The State of the Prisons.* London: J. M. Dent; New York: E. P. Dutton, 1929. First published in 1777.

Huxley, Aldous Leonard. *Brave New World.* Garden City, N.Y.: Doubleday, Doran & Co.; London: Chatto & Windus, 1932.

———. *Brave New World Revisited.* New York: Harper, 1958.

Irwin, John. *The Felon.* Englewood Cliffs, N.J.: Prentice-Hall, 1970.

Ives, George Cecil. *A History of Penal Methods: Criminals, Witches, Lunatics.* New York: F. A. Stokes, 1914.

Jackson, George. *Soledad Brother.* New York: Bantam Books, 1970.

Johnston, Norman. *The Human Cage: A Brief History of Prison Architecture.* New York: Walker, 1973.

Joint Commission on Correctional Manpower and Training. *Offenders as a Correctional Manpower Resource.* Washington, D.C.: Joint Commission on Correctional Manpower and Training, 1968.

Jones, Howard. *Crime in a Changing Society.* Baltimore: Penguin Books, 1965.

Jordan, Philip D. *Frontier Law and Order: Ten Essays.* Lincoln: University of Nebraska Press, 1970. The source cited for the Boston "people pen" of 1632 is Shurtleff, Nathaniel Bradstreet, ed. *Records of the Governor and Company of the Massachusetts Bay in New England, 1628–1686,* 1: 100. Boston: William White, 1853–54.

Kadish, Mortimer R., and Kadish, Sanford H. *Discretion to Disobey: A Study of Lawful Departures from Legal Rules.* Stanford: Stanford University Press, 1973.

Kadish, Sanford H. "The Decline of Innocence." *Cambridge Law Journal* 26 (1968): 273–90.

————. Review of Norval Morris and Howard Colin, *Studies in Criminal Law. Harvard Law Review* 78 (1965): 907–13.

Kafka, Franz. *The Penal Colony.* Translated by Willa and Edwin Muir. New York: Schocken, 1970.

Karp, David. *One.* New York: Vanguard, 1954.

Katz, Al. "Dangerousness: A Theoretical Reconstruction of the Criminal Law." *Buffalo Law Review* 19 (1969): 1–33, 603–40.

Kaufman, Irving R. "Prison: The Judge's Dilemma." *Fordham Law Review* 41 (1973): 495–516. Published concurrently in book form by Fordham University School of Law.

Keller, Oliver J., Jr., and Alper, Benedict S. *Halfway Houses: Community Centered Corrections and Treatment.* Lexington, Mass.: D. C. Heath, 1970.

Kittrie, Nicholas N. *The Right to Be Different: Deviance and Enforced Therapy.* Baltimore: Johns Hopkins Press, 1971.

Klare, Hugh John. *People in Prison.* London: Pitman, 1973.

Kozol, Harry L.; Boucher, Richard J.; and Garofalo, Ralph F. "The Diagnosis and Treatment of Dangerousness." *Crime and Delinquency* 18 (1972): 371–92.

Law Reform Commission of Canada. *The Principles of Sentencing and Dispositions: Working Paper No. 3.* Ottawa: Information Canada, 1974.

Levy, Howard, and Miller, David. *Going to Jail: The Political Prisoner.* New York: Grove Press, 1971.

Lewis, Clive Staples. "The Humanitarian Theory of Punishment."
    In C. S. Lewis, *God in the Dock: Essays on Theology and Ethics*.
    Edited by Walter Hooper. Grand Rapids, Mich.: Wm. B. Eerd-
    mans, 1970.
Lorenz, Konrad. *On Aggression*. Translated by Marjorie Kerr Wil-
    son. New York: Harcourt, Brace & World, 1966.
Luby, Elliot D., M.D., and Shuman, Samuel. *The Detroit Psycho-
    surgery Decision: The Judicial Practice of Medicine*. Forthcom-
    ing.
McKelvey, Blake. *American Prisons: A Study in American Social
    History prior to 1915*. Chicago: University of Chicago Press,
    1936.
Mannheim, Hermann. *Comparative Criminology: A Textbook*.
    London: Routledge & Kegan Paul, 1965. Vol. 2.
Mannheim, Hermann, ed. *Pioneers in Criminology*. London:
    Stevens, 1960.
Mannheim, Hermann, and Wilkins, Leslie T. *Prediction Methods
    in Relation to Borstal Training*. London: H. M. Stationery Office.
    1955.
Mark, V. H., and Ervin, F. R. *Violence and the Brain*. New York:
    Harper and Row, 1970.
Martin, John Bartlow. *Break Down the Walls: American Prisons,
    Present, Past, and Future*. New York: Ballantine Books, 1954.
Martinson, Robert. "What Works? Questions and Answers about
    Prison Reform." *The Public Interest*, No. 35 (1974): 22–54.
Massachusetts Correctional Association. *Correctional Reform: Illu-
    sion and Reality*. Prepared by Albert Morris. Correctional Re-
    search Series, Bulletin no. 22. Boston: Massachusetts Correc-
    tional Association, 1972.
Mattick, Hans W., and Aikman, Alexander B. "The Cloacal Region
    of American Corrections." *The Annals of the American Academy
    of Political and Social Science* 381 (1969): 109–18.
Mattick, Hans W., and Sweet, Ronald P. *Illinois Jails: Challenge
    and Opportunity for the 1970's*. Chicago: Center for Studies in
    Criminal Justice, University of Chicago, 1969.
Matza, David. *Becoming Deviant*. Englewood Cliffs, N.J.: Prentice-
    Hall, 1969.
Menninger, Karl, M.D. *The Crime of Punishment*. New York:
    Viking Press, 1966.
Mills, C. W. *Power, Politics and People*. New York: Oxford Uni-
    versity Press, 1963.
Minton, Robert. *Inside: Prison American Style*. New York: Ran-
    dom House, 1971.
Mitford, Jessica. *Kind and Unusual Punishment: The Prison Busi-
    ness*. New York: Alfred A. Knopf, 1973.
Moberly, Sir Walter. *The Ethics of Punishment*. London: Faber
    and Faber, 1968.

Morris, Norval. "Psychiatry and the Dangerous Criminal." *Southern California Law Review* 41 (1968): 514–47.

Morris, Norval, and Hawkins, Gordon. *The Honest Politician's Guide to Crime Control*. Chicago: University of Chicago Press, 1970.

Morris, Norval, and Howard, Colin. *Studies in Criminal Law*. Oxford: Clarendon Press, 1964.

Morris, Norval, and Mills, Michael. "Prisoners as Laboratory Animals." *Society*, July–August 1974.

————. "Prisoners as Laboratory Subjects." *Wall Street Journal*, April 2, 1974, p. 18.

Morris, Terence P. *Custodial Treatment of Offenders: Report of a Conference at Ditchley Park 27–30 April 1973*. Ditchley Paper No. 45. Ditchley Park, England: The Ditchley Foundation, 1973.

Motley, Constance Baker. " 'Law and Order' and the Criminal Justice System." *Journal of Criminal Law and Criminology* 64 (1973): 259–69.

Moyer, Frederic D., and Flynn, Edith E., eds. *Correctional Environments: A Summary of Recent Endeavors to Develop an Effective Correctional System Comprised of Programs and Environments Which Support and Encourage the Development of Full Citizenship*. Urbana, Ill.: National Clearinghouse for Correctional Programming and Architecture, University of Illinois, 1971.

Murphy, Jeffrie G., ed. *Punishment and Rehabilitation*. Basic Problems in Philosophy Series. Belmont, Calif.: Wadsworth, 1973.

Nagel, William G. *The New Red Barn: A Critical Look at the Modern American Prison*. New York: Walker, 1973.

National Advisory Commission on Criminal Justice Standards and Goals. *A National Strategy to Reduce Crime*. Washington, D.C.: U.S. Government Printing Office, 1973.

————. *Task Force Report: Corrections*. Washington, D.C.: U.S. Government Printing Office, 1973.

————. *Task Force Report: The Courts*. Chapter 3, "The Negotiated Plea." Washington, D.C.: U.S. Government Printing Office, 1973.

National Council on Crime and Delinquency. "The Nondangerous Offender Should Not Be Imprisoned: A Policy Statement." *Crime and Delinquency* 19 (1973): 449–56.

————. *Policies and Background Information: Institutional Construction, Compensation of Inmate Labor, The Federal Bureau of Prisons*. Washington, D.C.: National Council on Crime and Delinquency, 1972.

Newton, George D., and Zimring, Franklin E. *Firearms and Violence in American Life*. Staff Report to the National Commission on the Causes and Prevention of Violence, vol. 7. Washington, D.C.: U.S. Government Printing Office, 1969.

Ohlin, Lloyd E. "Correctional Strategies in Conflict." *Proceedings of the American Philosophical Society* 118 (1974): 248–53.

Ohlin, Lloyd E., and Remington, F. J. "Sentencing Structure: Its Effect upon Systems for the Administration of Criminal Justice." *Law and Contemporary Problems* 23 (1958): 495–507.

Orwell, George. *Animal Farm.* New York: Harcourt Brace Jovanovich, 1946.

———. *1984.* New York: Harcourt Brace Jovanovich, 1949.

Packer, Herbert L. *The Limits of the Criminal Sanction.* Stanford: Stanford University Press, 1969.

———. "Making the Punishment Fit the Crime." *Harvard Law Review* 77 (1964): 1071–82.

Palmer, Larry I. "A Model of Criminal Dispositions: An Alternative to Official Discretion in Sentencing." *Georgetown Law Journal* 62 (1973): 1–59.

President's Commission on Law Enforcement and Administration of Justice. *The Challenge of Crime in a Free Society.* Washington, D.C.: U.S. Government Printing Office, 1967.

———. *Task Force Report: Corrections.* Washington, D.C.: U.S. Government Printing Office, 1968.

Pugh, Ralph Bernard. *Imprisonment in Medieval England.* London: Cambridge University Press, 1968.

Quinney, Richard. *Crime and Justice in Society.* Boston: Little, Brown, 1969.

———. *The Social Reality of Crime.* Boston: Little, Brown, 1970.

Radzinowicz, Leon. *In Search of Criminology.* London: Heinemann; Cambridge, Mass.: Harvard University Press, 1962.

Radzinowicz, Leon, and Wolfgang, Marvin E., eds. *Crime and Justice.* Vols. 1–3. New York: Basic Books, 1971.

Rawls, John. *A Theory of Justice.* Cambridge, Mass.: Belknap Press of Harvard University Press, 1971.

Reckless, Walter C. *The Crime Problem.* 5th ed. New York: Meredith, 1973.

Reisner, Ralph. "Psychiatric Hospitalization and the Constitution: Some Observations on Emerging Trends." *University of Illinois Law Forum* 1973: 9–20.

Report of the President's Commission on Crime in the District of Columbia. Washington, D.C.: U.S. Government Printing Office, 1966.

Robinson, James, and Smith, Gerald. "The Effectiveness of Correctional Programs." *Crime and Delinquency* 17 (1971): 67–80.

Roosenburg, Anne-Marie. "The Interaction between Prisoners, Victims and Their Social Networks." In *Medical Care of Prisoners and Detainees.* Ciba Foundation Symposium 16. Amsterdam: Associated Scientific Publishers, 1973.

Rothman, David J. "Decarcerating Prisoners and Patients." *Civil Liberties Review* 1 (1973): 8–30.

———. *The Discovery of the Asylum: Social Order and Disorder in the New Republic.* Boston: Little, Brown, 1971.

Rubin, Bernard. "Prediction of Dangerousness in Mentally Ill Criminals." *Archives of General Psychiatry* 27 (1972): 397–407.

Rubin, Sol, et al. *The Law of Criminal Correction.* St. Paul: West Publishing Co., 1963.

Rusche, Georg, and Kirchheimer, Otto. *Punishment and Social Structure.* New York: Columbia University Press, 1939.

Russell, Bertrand. *Power.* New York: Norton, 1938.

Saleebey, George. "Youth Correctional Centers: A New Approach to Treating Youthful Offenders." *Federal Probation* 34 (1970): 49–53.

Schrag, Clarence. *Crime and Justice: American Style.* Crime and Delinquency Issues: A Monograph Series. Rockville, Md.: National Institute of Mental Health, Center for Studies of Crime and Delinquency, 1971.

Schur, Edwin M. *Crimes without Victims: Deviant Behavior and Public Policy.* Englewood Cliffs, N.J.: Prentice-Hall, 1965.

———. *Our Criminal Society.* Englewood Cliffs, N.J.: Prentice-Hall, 1969.

———. *Radical Nonintervention: Rethinking the Delinquency Problem.* Englewood Cliffs, N.J.: Prentice-Hall, 1973.

Sellin, Thorsten. *Pioneering in Penology: The Amsterdam Houses of Correction in the 16th and 17th Centuries.* Philadelphia: University of Pennsylvania Press; London: H. Milford, Oxford University Press, 1944.

Simon, Rita James. *The Jury and the Defense of Sanity.* Boston: Little, Brown, 1967.

Singer, Richard G. "Sending Men to Prison: Constitutional Aspects of the Burden of Proof and the Doctrine of the Least Drastic Alternative as Applied to Sentencing Determinations." *Cornell Law Review* 58 (1972): 51–89.

Solzhenitsyn, Aleksandr I. *The Gulag Archipelago: An Experiment in Literary Investigation.* Translated by Thomas P. Whitney. New York: Harper & Row, 1973.

Spaeth, Edmund B., Jr. "A Response to *Struggle for Justice.*" *Prison Journal* 52 (1972): 4–32. See also Greenberg, David F.

Steadman, Henry J., and Cocozza, Joseph J. *Careers of the Criminally Insane.* Forthcoming.

Steadman, Henry J., and Keveles, Gary. "The Community Adjustment and Criminal Activity of the Baxstrom Patients: 1966–70." *American Journal of Psychiatry* 129 (1972): 304–10.

Storr, Anthony. *Human Aggression.* New York: Atheneum, 1968.

————. *Human Destructiveness.* The Columbus Centre Series: Studies in the Dynamics of Persecution and Extermination. Edited by Norman Cohn. New York: Basic Books, 1972.

Studt, Elliot; Messinger, Sheldon L.; and Wilson, Thomas P. *C-Unit: Search for Community in Prison.* New York: Russell Sage Foundation, 1968.

Stürup, Georg K., M.D. *Treating the "Untreatable": Chronic Criminals at Herstedvester.* Baltimore: Johns Hopkins Press, 1968.

Sutherland, Edwin Hardin, and Cressey, Donald R. *Criminology.* 8th ed. Philadelphia: Lippincott, 1970.

Sykes, Gresham M. *Crime and Society.* New York: Random House, 1967.

————. *The Society of Captives.* Princeton, N.J.: Princeton University Press, 1958.

Szasz, Thomas Stephen. *Law, Liberty and Psychiatry: An Inquiry into the Social Uses of Mental Health Practices.* New York: Macmillan, 1963.

————. *The Myth of Mental Illness.* New York: Harper & Row, 1961.

————. *Psychiatric Justice.* New York: Macmillan, 1965.

Tappan, Paul Wilbur. *Crime, Justice, and Correction.* New York: McGraw-Hill, 1960.

Teeters, Negley King. *The Cradle of the Penitentiary: The Walnut Street Jail at Philadelphia, 1773–1835.* Philadelphia: Pennsylvania Prison Society, 1955.

Vera Institute of Justice. *The Manhattan Court Employment Project: Summary Report on Phase One—November 1, 1967–October 3, 1969.* New York: Vera Institute of Justice, 1970.

Vold, George Bryan. *Prediction Methods and Parole: A Study of Factors Involved in the Violation or Non-Violation of Parole in a Group of Minnesota Adult Males.* Minneapolis: Sociological Press, 1931.

————. *Theoretical Criminology.* New York: Oxford University Press, 1958.

Walker, Nigel. *Crime and Punishment in Britain: An Analysis of the Penal System in Theory, Law, and Practice.* 2d rev. ed. Edinburgh: Edinburgh University Press, 1968.

————. *Crimes, Courts and Figures: An Introduction to Criminal Statistics.* Harmondsworth, England: Penguin Books, 1971.

————. *Sentencing in a Rational Society.* London: Allen Lane, Penguin Press, 1969.

Ward, Paul G., and Woods, Greg D. *Law and Order in Australia.* Sydney: Angus and Robertson, 1972.

Wenk, E.; Robinson, J.; and Smith, G. "Can Violence Be Predicted?" *Crime and Delinquency* 18 (1972): 393–402. See too the excellent study of this whole problem by Gilbert Geis and John Monahan, "The Social Ecology of Violence," in *Man and*

Morality, edited by T. Lickona. New York: Holt, Rinehart and Winston, in press.

West, Donald James. *The Habitual Prisoner: An Enquiry by the Cambridge Institute of Criminology*. London: Macmillan; New York: St. Martin's Press, 1963.

————. *The Young Offender*. Harmondsworth, England: Penguin; New York: International Universities Press, 1967.

West, Donald James, ed. *The Future of Parole: Commentaries on Systems in Britain and U.S.A.* London: Duckworth, 1972.

Wheeler, Stanton. *Controlling Delinquents*. New York: Wiley, 1968.

Wilkins, Leslie T. "Crime and Criminal Justice at the Turn of the Century." Paper presented at the 77th Annual Meeting of the American Academy of Political and Social Science, Philadelphia, April 1973.

————. *Crime and the Tender-Minded: A Packaged Philosophy*. Community Education Series 1, no. 1. Toronto: John Howard Society of Ontario, n.d.

————. "Directions for Corrections." *Proceedings of the American Philosophical Society* 118 (1974): 235–47.

————. *Evaluation of Penal Measures*. New York: Random House, 1969.

————. *Social Deviance: Social Policy, Action and Research*. Englewood Cliffs, N.J.: Prentice-Hall, 1964.

Williams, Glanville Llewelyn. *The Sanctity of Life and the Criminal Law*. New York: Alfred A. Knopf, 1957.

Wines, Frederick Howard. *Punishment and Reformation: A Study of the Penitentiary System*. New York: T. Y. Crowell, 1910.

Wolfgang, Marvin E.; Savitz, Leonard; and Johnston, Norman. *The Sociology of Crime and Delinquency*. 2d ed. New York: Wiley, 1970.

Wootton, Barbara. *Crime and the Criminal Law: Reflections of a Magistrate and Social Scientist*. London: Stevens & Sons, 1963.

————. *Social Science and Social Pathology*. London: G. Allen & Unwin, 1959.

Zimring, Franklin E. "The Court Employment Project." Unpublished report to the New York City Human Resources Administration, 1973.

————. "Measuring the Impact of Pretrial Diversion from the Criminal Justice System." *University of Chicago Law Review* 41 (1974): 224–41.

————. *Perspectives on Deterrence*. Crime and Delinquency Issues: A Monograph Series. Chevy Chase, Md.: National Institute of Mental Health, Center for Studies of Crime and Delinquency, 1971.

————. "Threat of Punishment as an Instrument of Crime Control." *Proceedings of the American Philosophical Society* 118 (1974): 231–34.

Zimring, Franklin E., and Hawkins, Gordon. "Deterrence and
    Marginal Groups." *Journal of Research in Crime and Delin-
    quency* 5 (1968): 100–14.
Zimring, Franklin E., and Hawkins, Gordon. *Deterrence: The Legal
    Threat in Crime Control.* Chicago: University of Chicago Press,
    1973.

Index

Index